100 JAZZ ROCK
FUSION LICKS FOR GUITAR

Discover the Language & Techniques of the World's Greatest Fusion Guitarists

NICK MELLOR

100 Jazz-Rock Fusion Licks for Guitar

Discover the Language & Techniques of the World's Greatest Fusion Guitarists

ISBN: 978-1-78933-430-2

Published by **www.fundamental-changes.com**

Copyright © 2024 Nick Mellor

Edited by Joseph Alexander

The moral right of this author has been asserted.

All rights reserved. No part of this publication may be reproduced, stored in a retrieval system, or transmitted in any form or by any means, without the prior permission in writing from the publisher.

The publisher is not responsible for websites (or their content) that are not owned by the publisher.

www.fundamental-changes.com

For over 350 free guitar lessons with videos check out:

www.fundamental-changes.com

Join our free Facebook Community of Cool Musicians

www.facebook.com/groups/fundamentalguitar

Tag us for a share on Instagram: **FundamentalChanges**

Cover Image Copyright: Shutterstock

Contents

About the Author 4

Introduction 5

Get the Audio 6

Chapter One: Mike Stern 7

Chapter Two: Pat Metheny 16

Chapter Three: John Scofield 23

Chapter Four: Robben Ford 30

Chapter Five: Larry Carlton 38

Chapter Six: Allan Holdsworth 46

Chapter Seven: John McLaughlin 55

Chapter Eight: Wayne Krantz 63

Chapter Nine: Jimmy Herring 71

Chapter Ten: Fusion Over II-V-Is 80

Conclusion 90

About the Author

Nick Mellor is a session guitarist, writer and teacher based in the Midlands and Northwest of England.

He picked up the guitar in the early 1980s and in 2002 won *Guitarist* magazine's Guitarist of The Year competition which was judged Guthrie Govan. Since then, he has continued to play sessions and gigs all over the UK as well as overseas.

Educated at St. Anne's, Oxford, Nick achieved his BA in English Language and Literature in 1993. He currently holds a position as a lecturer in Jazz and Rock Guitar/Performance Studies at Salford University.

* * *

Fundamental Changes has published over 300 music tuition books in four languages and is currently accepting submissions from prospective authors and teachers of all instruments. Get in touch via the **www.fundamental-changes.com** if you'd like to work with us on a project.

Introduction

In some quarters, Jazz-Rock Fusion was once regarded as an inferior offshoot of Jazz – a crass commercialisation of a tradition known for its subtlety, elegance and integrity. This misconception has gradually been dismantled over the last four decades, as great musicians like Chick Corea, Herbie Hancock, John Scofield and John McLaughlin, among others, have explored its endless potential. These players have created a legacy of creative music at the highest levels, incorporating classical harmony, exotic rhythms, virtuoso musicianship, extended improvisations and electronic textures.

This book distils the styles and techniques of nine guitar players central to the genre.

The licks that follow are not for the faint-hearted, nor for the beginner, and are intended for intermediate to advanced players with a good technical grounding in a range of scales and techniques.

While I've kept this book "theory-lite", a grounding in intervallic relationships and an understanding of Major, Minor, Dominant 7th and Diminished chords, along with the main tonalities of Major, Harmonic Minor, Melodic Minor, Diminished and Whole Tone, will be helpful to fully appreciate the harmonic contexts in which the lines are played.

Given that the guitar is a visual, shape-orientated instrument, it's still relatively easy to find your way around most of these complex lines as the licks often fit around common shapes that allow for seamless assimilation into your vocabulary.

In each chapter, various scales, concepts and melodic cells are presented in the first few examples to help you extract some key elements from each player's style. Then, in the ten licks that follow you will see how longer lines can be constructed by combining and embellishing these building blocks. Each lick is presented in the key of G to allow easy comparison between the styles of the different players. I recommend that you learn these in other keys as well, to help cement the sound under your fingers. To help you incorporate them into your vocabulary more naturally, it will help you to organise them around CAGED or Pentatonic positions where appropriate.

This book is aimed at Rock, Blues and Jazz players who want to incorporate some Fusion ideas into their playing. It should help you to step outside the traditional language of these genres and gain some new ideas and inspiration. However, there's also plenty of ideas to teach the seasoned Fusion player a few new tricks!

I hope you enjoy playing these licks as much as I did writing them.

Good luck!

Nick Mellor

Get the Audio

The audio files for this book are available to download for free from **www.fundamental-changes.com**. The link is in the top right-hand corner. Click "Download Audio" and choose your instrument. Select the title of this book from the menu, and complete the form to get your audio.

We recommend that you download the files directly to your computer (not to your tablet or phone) and extract them there before adding them to your media library. If you encounter any difficulty, we provide technical support within 24 hours via the contact form.

For over 350 free guitar lessons with videos check out:

www.fundamental-changes.com

Join our free Facebook Community of Cool Musicians

www.facebook.com/groups/fundamentalguitar

Tag us for a share on Instagram: **FundamentalChanges**

Chapter One: Mike Stern

Mike Stern was born in Boston in 1953, grew up in Washington DC, and attended the Berklee College of Music in the early 1970s. After leaving Berklee, Stern joined the band Blood, Sweat and Tears in 1973, touring and playing on two albums. After leaving, he spent two years with Billy Cobham from 1979.

Stern was asked to join Miles Davis' comeback band in 1981 for the album, *The Man With The Horn*. His face-melting solo on the opening track, *Fat Time*, announced the arrival of an aggressive new Fusion shredder on the scene.

Stern spent two years with Miles and his solo career didn't launch properly until 1986, when he released *Upside Downside*. The album set the formula for Stern's subsequent career. High energy Fusion, heart-wrenching ballads, Metheny-esque "heartland" music and Weather Report-style "world" influences were all combined through Stern's considerable compositional skill and authoritative playing.

He followed this with four decades of finely-crafted albums featuring musicians such as Jim Beard, Bob Berg, Peter Erskine, Dave Weckl, Dennis Chambers and many other top-flight musicians. Highlights of his discography are *Is What It Is*, *Play* (featuring Bill Frisell and John Scofield) and *Who Let The Cats Out?*

Stern creates a heavily modulated tone with his rack-mounted Yamaha SPX90 and its infamous "symphonic" pitch shifter effect, which gives his guitar a thick, almost three-dimensional timbre – a sound he has stuck with for over four decades.

He favours telecaster-type guitars. After using vintage Fenders in the early part of his career, he switched to his signature Yamaha Pacifica model with Seymour Duncan pickups.

Our first four examples are short *melodic cells*. These are small building blocks or motifs that are repeated, modified and linked together to create longer lines. These four short examples are based around the G Dorian scale. Play through these fragments several times to internalise them and prepare for the more complex, longer lines later.

Example 1a is a G Dorian melodic cell used in both Jazz and Rock in equal measure.

Example 1a:

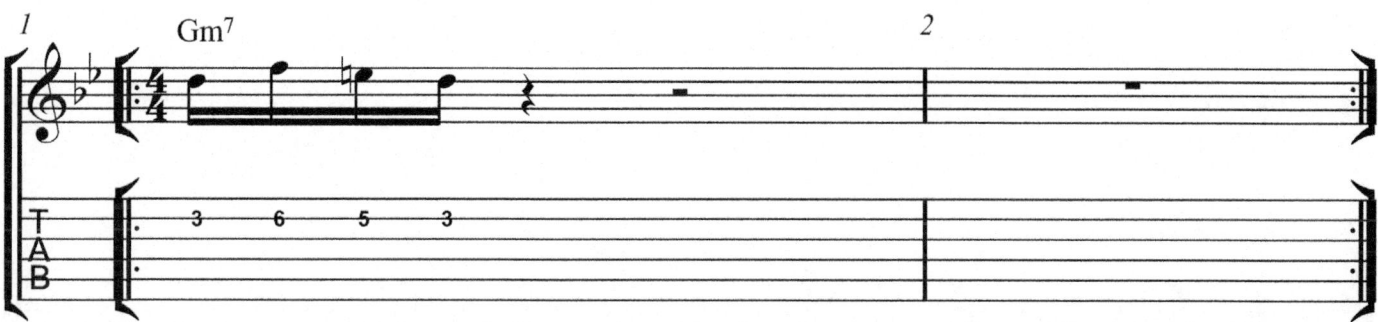

The next fragment introduces *colour tones* and non-scale tones by adding chromatic notes. This idea starts on the b5 (Eb) and works its way down to the 4th (C) via the G Whole Tone scale. Slide from the 3rd to the 2nd fret with your first finger.

Example 1b:

This fragment begins on the b5 (Db) and moves up to the natural 5th and b7 before making a chromatic descent, alternating between the 5th and the three notes above it. This could be seen as an embellished *enclosure* of the final D note, where we begin a half-step below the target note, then play a sequence of notes above until finally descending to the targeted D again.

Example 1c:

The final melodic cell is a bebop cliché often used by Stern. The line starts on the 4th of the scale, descends chromatically to the 3rd, then returns to the 4th before ending on the 2nd (A). The exact same pattern would also work descending from the root note (G) to the 6th.

Example 1d:

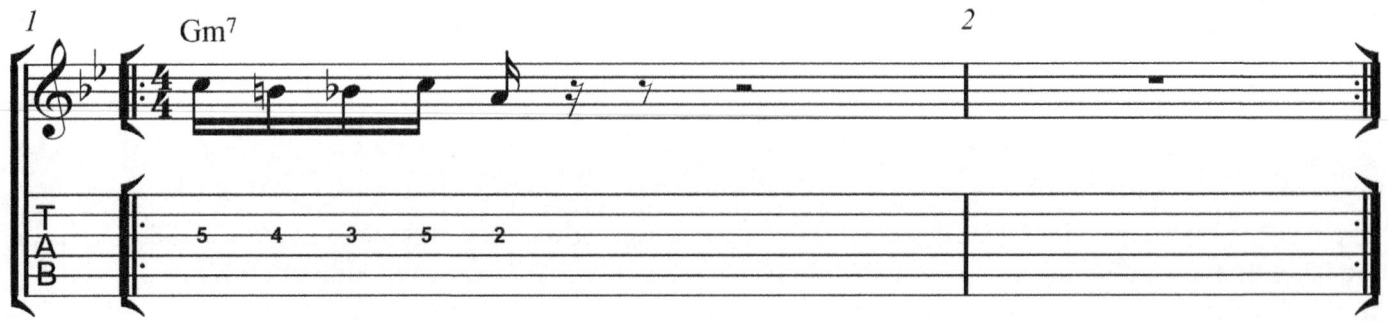

Now let's use these cells to build some longer licks.

This idea begins with a simple four-note cell which descends chromatically. As we descend, we introduce slight variations to the original three-note arrangement. For instance, the cell on beats 3 and 4 resembles Example 1a.

The lick continues in this fashion until we reach shape one of G Minor Pentatonic where it descends across the strings outlining a Bb Augmented triad, which is contained within the G Melodic Minor scale. The line ends on the 9th (A).

Example 1e:

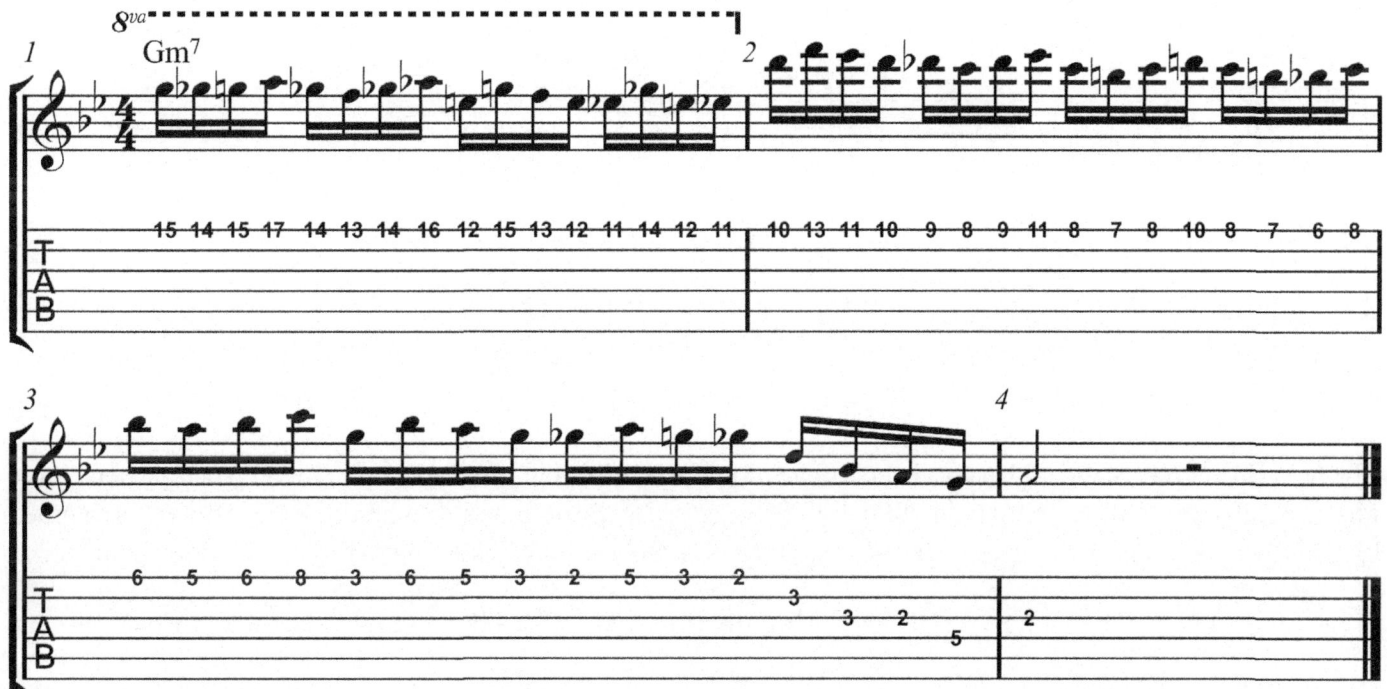

Example 1f starts in a similar way but moves vertically rather than horizontally. As the line descends, notes are added from G Harmonic Minor (F# and Eb). In the final bar, we move seamlessly into an ascending D Half-Whole Diminished scale run starting at the 10th fret on the D string. The line resolves with a classic blues lick in true Stern style.

Example 1f:

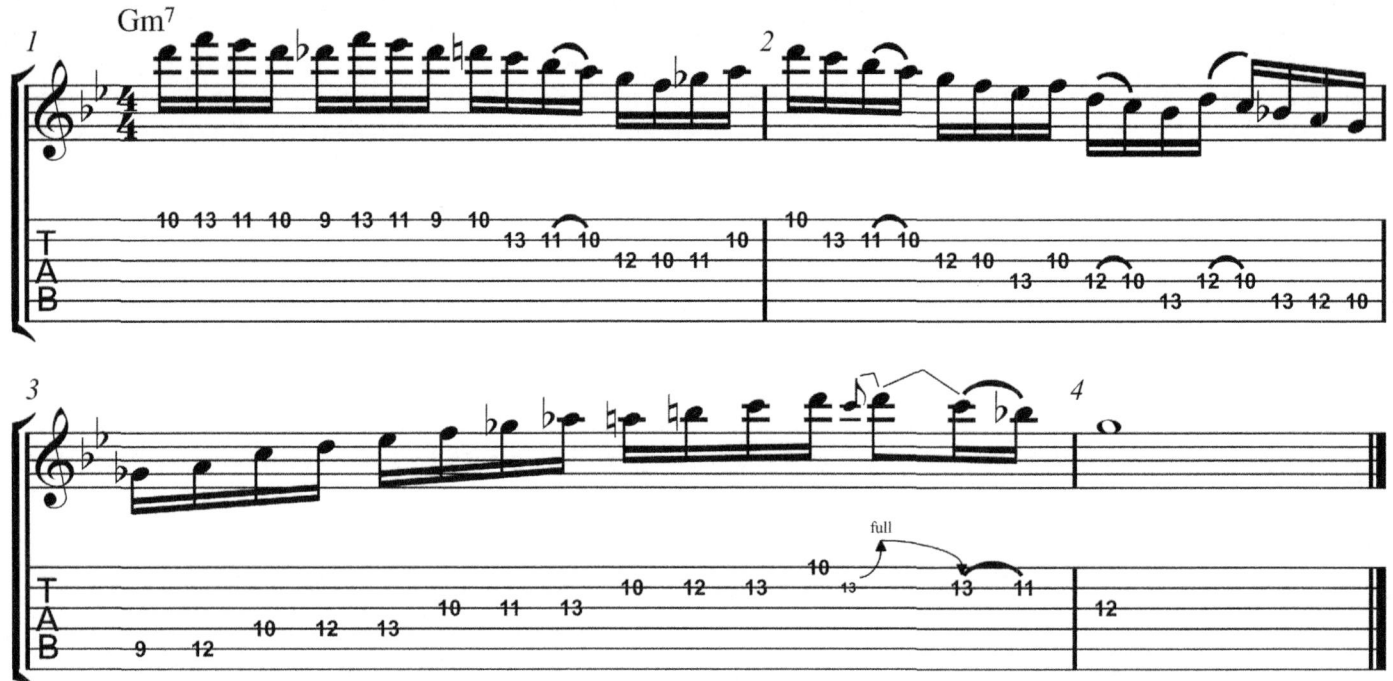

The next line explores the highest registers of the guitar as a G Dorian run leads to the high E string where some familiar cells and motifs are played. Notice the enclosure on beats 3 and 4, where the b3 (Bb) is surrounded by a chromatic motif. The second bar *side-steps* into G# Dorian before landing safely in G Minor on beat 3.

It ends with a G Natural Minor/G Harmonic Minor hybrid scale with a bebop-style leap of a 6th.

Example 1g:

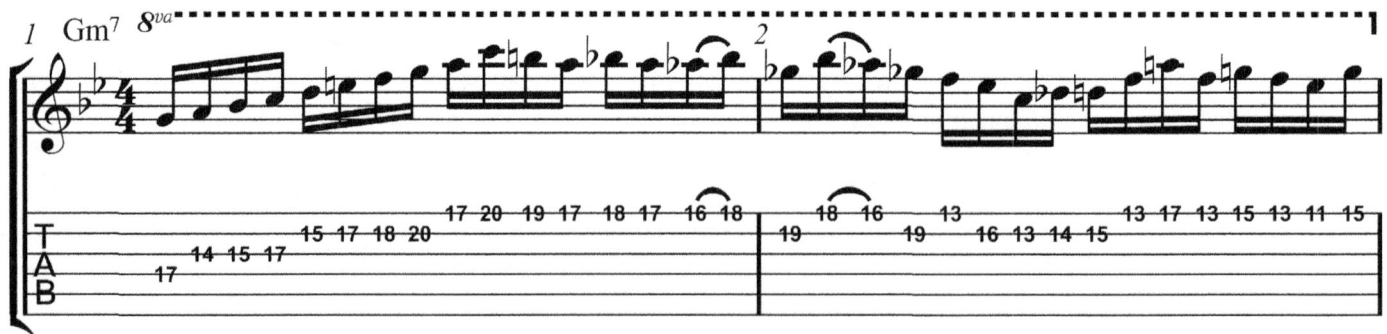

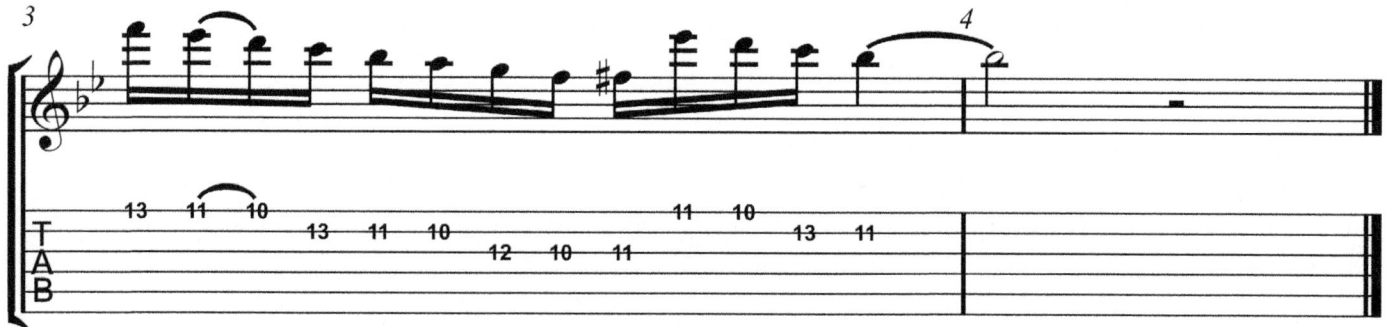

Example 1h uses enclosure and chromaticism in G Dorian and changes position half-way through the first bar, before shifting to G Melodic Minor ideas with chromaticism in bar two. The slurred movement from the 4th to the 3rd fret in bar one should be played with the first finger to add variety to the articulation and allow the phrases to breathe. Once again, the tension is resolved by a bluesy pentatonic phrase.

Example 1h:

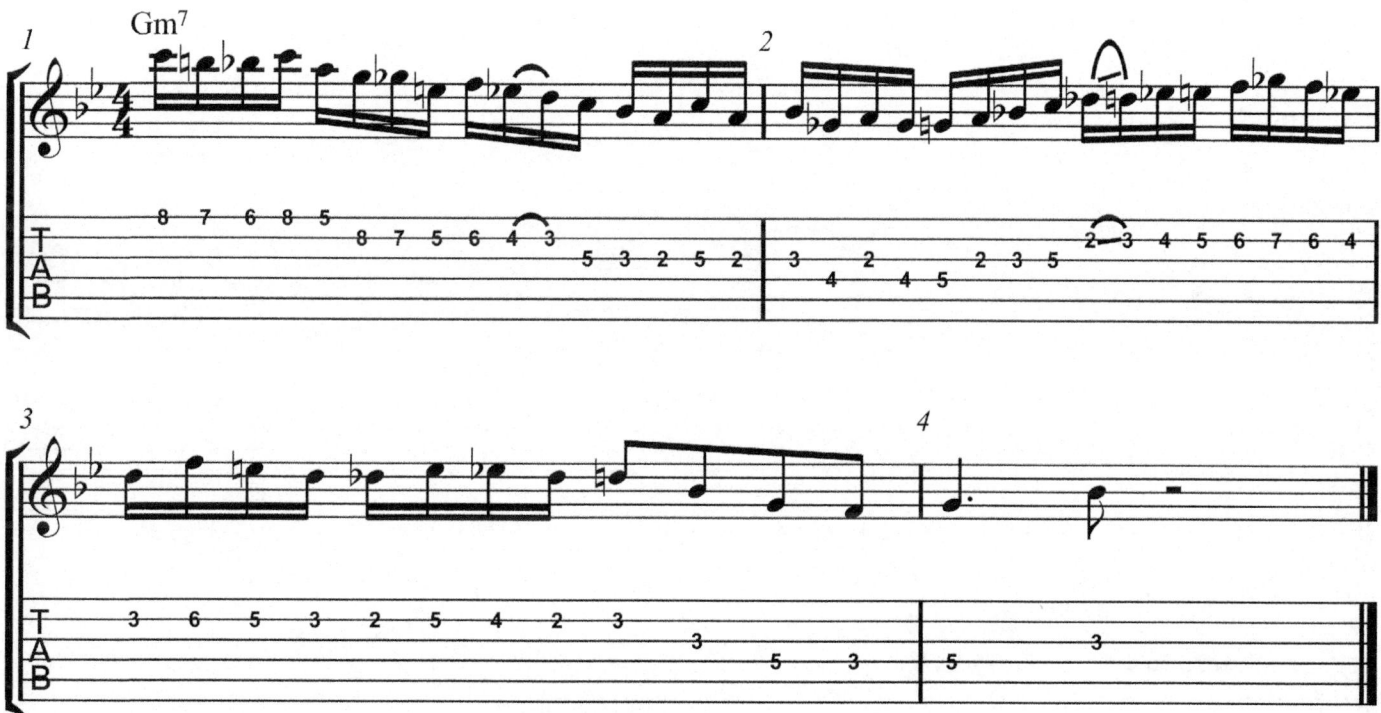

The next example sandwiches a conventional scale run between two blues phrases, shooting for a "heavy metal bebop" approach. Note the subtle use of space after the long, dense "sheets of sound" of previous examples.

The pickup at the end of bar two takes us into an ascending G Melodic Minor run that ends with a combination of half- and whole-step bends, suggesting classic blues but retaining a modal sound with the half-step bend in the penultimate bar.

Example 1i:

Example 1j begins with a half-step bend from the 6th to the b7, before mixing G Dorian and G Harmonic Minor scale runs. The D Major triad outlined in the second bar, followed by an F natural, suggests the C Diminished scale.

One stylistic trait here is the repetition of a note, sometimes called "double noting". This adds rhythmic interest and is a technique often used by both Jim Hall and Pat Metheny (both strong influences on Stern). The movement from F# to G at the end implies a V-I resolution of D Major to G Minor.

Example 1j:

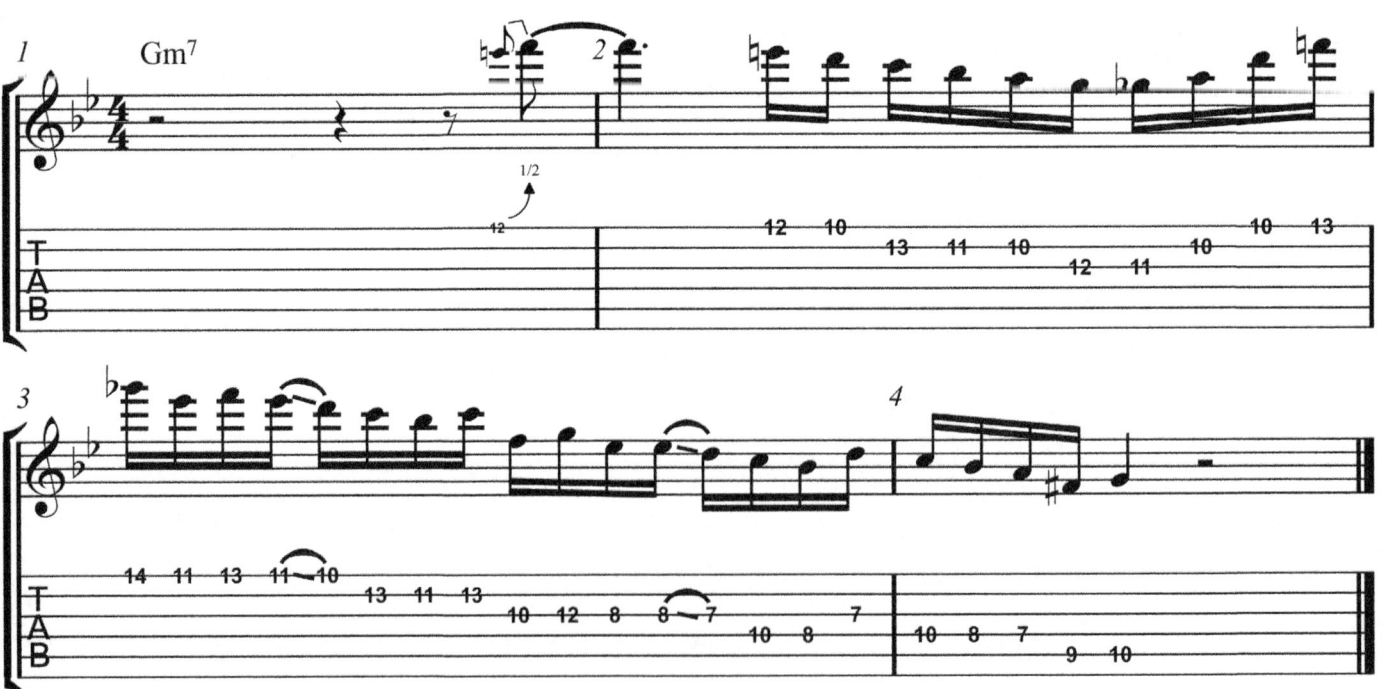

Next, D Harmonic Minor is used against the G Minor harmony to create a Dorian #4 sound (G Dorian with a C# instead of a C).

The second bar features a one-octave chromatic scale starting on E. The A Major triad on the final beat of bar two is moved up chromatically to eventually become C Major, a common superimposition over G Dorian.

Example 1k:

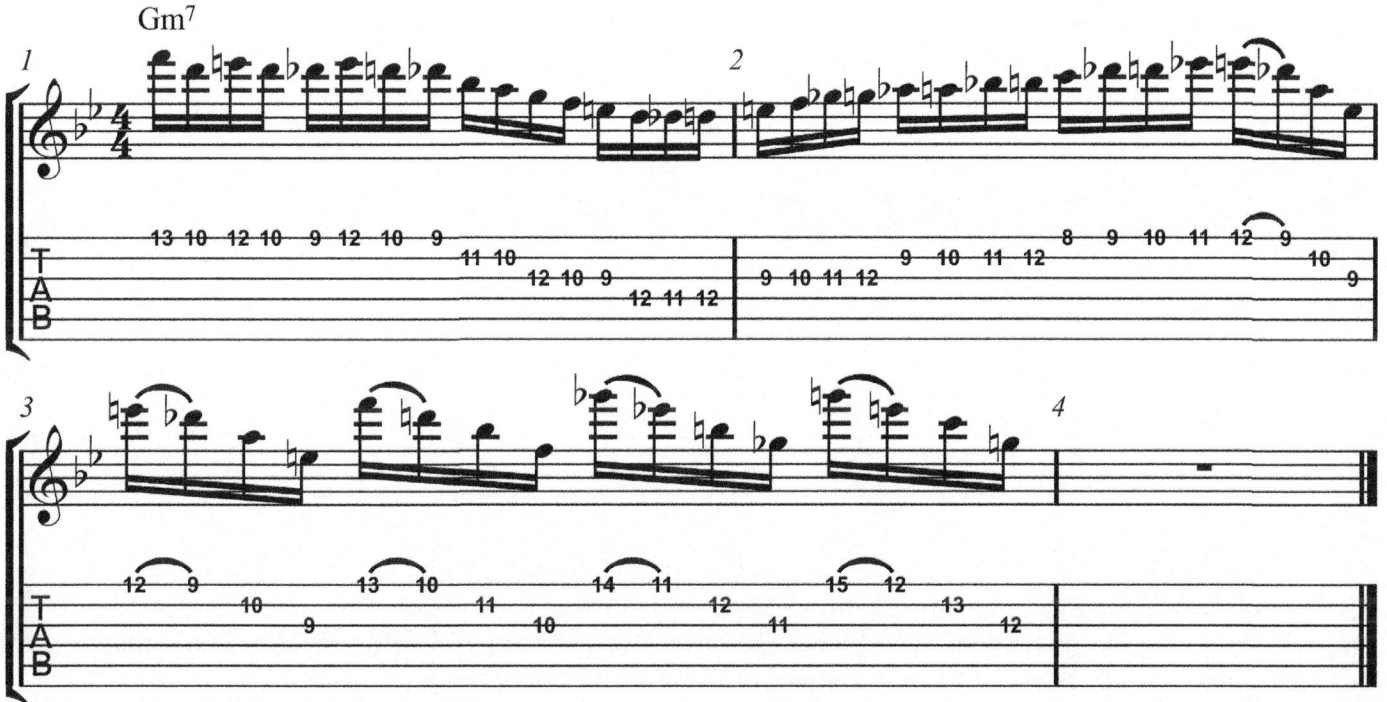

A traditional bebop structure is "arpeggio ascending, scale descending" but in Example 1l we reverse that concept. I begin with a descending FMaj7 arpeggio which emphasises the natural 6 (E) and b7 (F).

Notice the triplet 1/16ths played using a reverse sweep. This FMaj7 arpeggio is followed by an ascending G Dorian run with chromatic passing notes. The triad shape idea from the previous example is used again but notice how the Gm6 arpeggio is played as a colourful alternative in the final bar.

Example 1l:

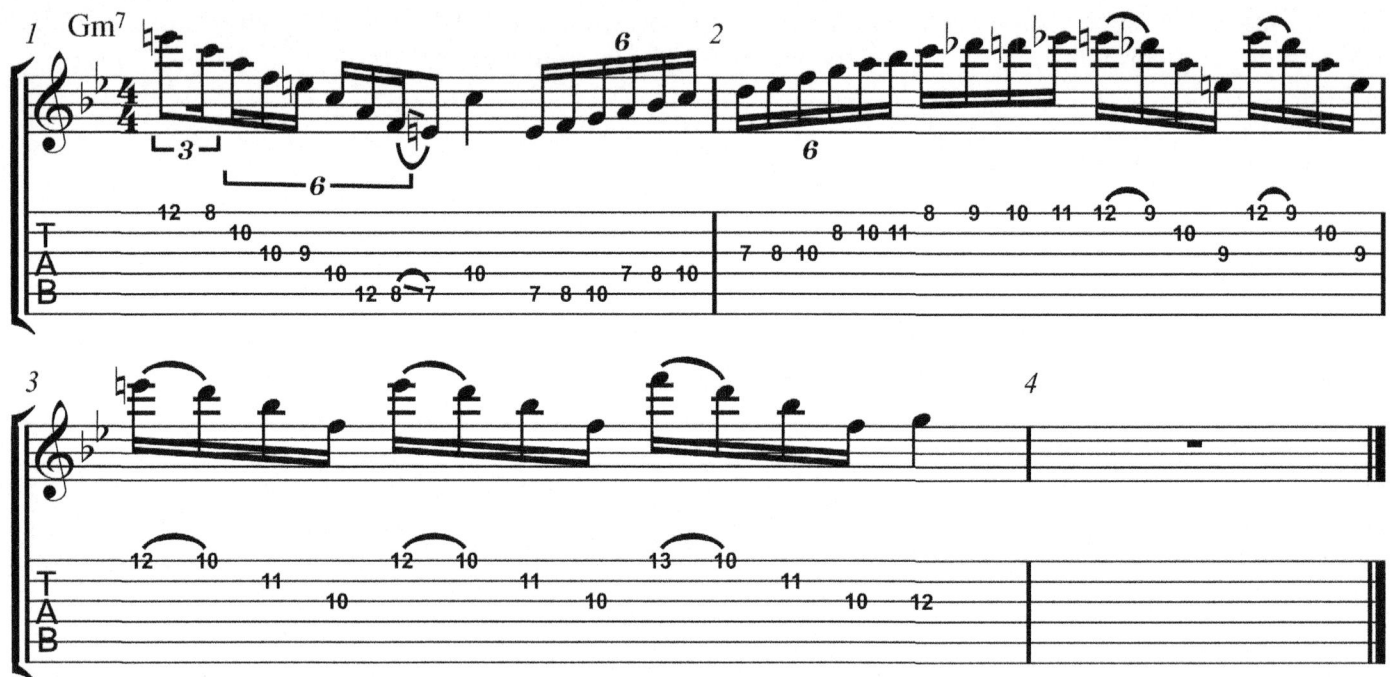

Example 1m begins outside the key of G Minor in Eb Dorian before returning inside via the enclosure on beat 2 of bar two. We could come up with a complex analysis of this harmony, but the outside sound is simply created by moving our hand a half-step higher. To finish, we play some "joining-the-dots" chromaticism by linking fragments of G Dorian, G Minor Pentatonic and G Harmonic Minor.

Example 1m:

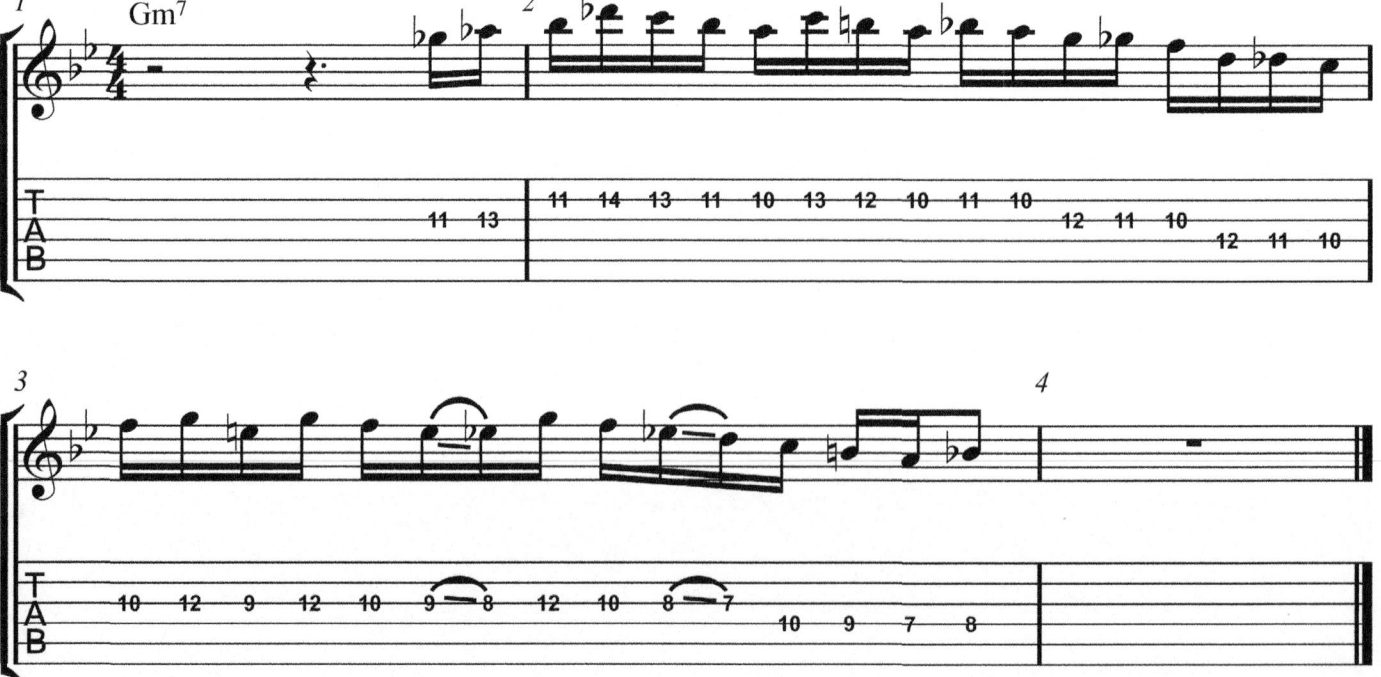

The final Mike Stern style line uses a BbMaj7 arpeggio as a launch pad into a four-note Bb Melodic Minor motif. This is moved up the fretboard into three different positions that suggests D, G and Bb Harmonic/Melodic Minor respectively, to bring out different tensions on each modulation. Notice the rhythmic displacement created as the four-note motif begins on a different beat as it ascends.

Example 1n:

Chapter Two: Pat Metheny

Pat Metheny was born in Lee's Summit, Missouri in 1954 and grew up surrounded by music as his grandfather, father and older brother all played the trumpet. After briefly exploring the trumpet, Metheny broke with family tradition, took up guitar at the age of 12, and was playing professional Jazz gigs by age 15.

Metheny was offered a place at the University of Miami where he was immediately given the role of tutor. Soon after moving to Berklee, Metheny forged relationships with Mick Goodrick, Gary Burton and Jaco Pastorius. Metheny recorded *Ring* with Gary Burton in 1974 for the ECM label, which in turn led to the recording of his own debut album, *Bright Size Life* a year later.

He quickly built on this acclaimed debut, forming the Pat Metheny Group with Lyle Mays, and recorded three ground-breaking albums that further established the band's reputation. *Watercolours*, *Pat Metheny Group* and *American Garage* all appeared in quick succession from 1977 to 1979.

Metheny returned to his Jazz roots with *80/81* in 1980 featuring Jack Dejohnette and Michael Brecker. The influence of Ornette Coleman featuring prominently, as it would continue to do so throughout his career. The 1980s saw Metheny become a Jazz and Fusion supremo with a string of albums that included 1982's Grammy winning *Offramp*, the live double album *Travels* (1983) and *First Circle* (1984). The band recorded a further eight albums over the next two decades after a move to the Geffen label in 1986, which allowed them creative freedom.

At the heart of Metheny's sound is the Gibson ES-175 which he used for the best part of two decades. When this guitar started to wear out through constant touring, he eventually collaborated with Ibanez to make an ES-175 style instrument that is virtually indistinguishable in timbre from the Gibson on which it is modelled.

In the '70s and '80s, Metheny used chorus, pitch shifting, delays and digital reverbs to sculpt a sound that was in keeping with the sonic trends of the era. His sonic exploration continued into the '90s and '00s with the 42-string Pikasso guitar and his use of a Roland guitar synthesizer.

Metheny's style is complex and articulate but the licks in this chapter will give you a starting point to help get inside his approach. We will begin with some short melodic cells that are analysed as Bb Major lines but work equally well over the relative G Minor.

Example 2a starts on the b7 of Bb and acts as a lead-in note to the major 7th (A) which is the first target note. The cell then descends chromatically to the 5th (F). Notice how the dissonant notes fall on weak beats and consonant ones fall on strong beats.

When played over a Gm7, this line targets the 9th (A) and b7th (F), and highlights some interesting musical colours.

Example 2a:

Next is a two-note chromatic move across two strings that can be heard in the playing of Wes Montgomery and Pat Martino. It is a useful fragment for shifting between and connecting positions, and is essentially an enclosure of the target Bb note.

Example 2b:

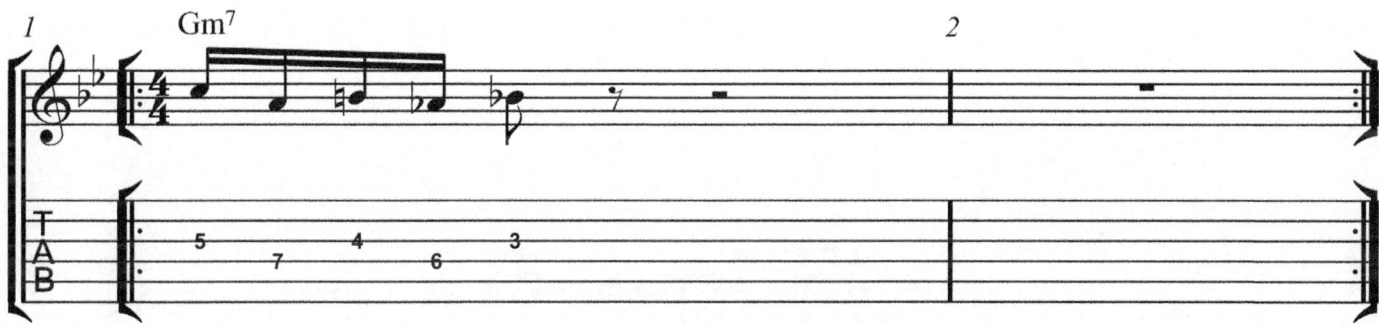

Example 2c again targets chord tones, this time the 9th, 3rd and 5th. Metheny superimposes this idea over altered dominant chords by starting the motif on the #5.

Example 2c:

The final fragment combines pentatonic scales, chord tones and chromaticism to present a microcosm of Metheny's playing in a single eleven note-run. The line starts on the 7th of Bb Major (A), moves to the 9th (C) to enclose the Bb at the 6th fret before descending through D Minor pentatonic. It finishes with the approach pattern from Example 2b.

Example 2d:

Example 2e is a largely diatonic BbMaj7 arpeggio with passing tones played over a Gm7 chord – a common substitution. It begins as an arpeggio but becomes more scalic as it ascends. Use pull-offs when descending to create a semi-legato effect on the D Minor Pentatonic phrase. The chromatically descending 3rds from Example 2b complete the line which resolves to the G root note.

Example 2e:

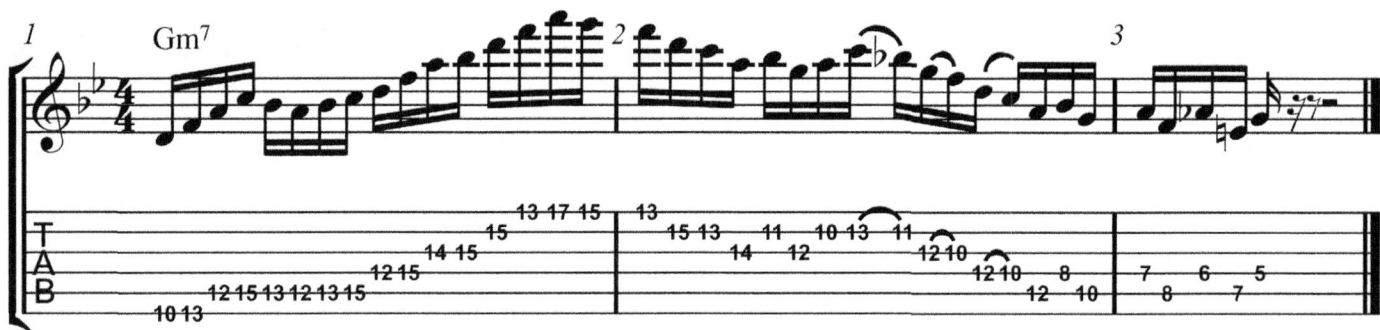

The following idea is a longer and more complex line with a Dorian flavour due to the natural 6th (E) but there are hints of D Minor Pentatonic. Pay attention to the chromatic connecting notes on the G string. We finish with a traditional bebop enclosure surrounding the 4th (C).

Example 2f:

Example 2g begins with the motif from Example 2a before slipping and sliding through different positions as it descends. It incorporates all four of the melodic cells and ends with a *shell voicing* (a chord voicing consisting of root, 3rd and 7th), which is a moveable shape often used by Metheny.

Example 2g:

The next idea contains a great deal of chromaticism in the 5th position and uses all four melodic cells from examples 2a-2d. The use of Example 2b on the lower strings at the end is a classic Metheny trope.

Example 2h:

Example 2i further explores the movable shell voicing approach. It starts on a Dm7 shell voicing that moves through Em7, FMaj7 and F#Maj7 before ending on Am7. Try this with strict alternate picking or hybrid picking. The lower note could be played with a "hammer-on from nowhere". This idea is so important it is sometimes referred to as "the Metheny lick".

Example 2i:

In Example 2j we solo over a static G7 chord. The leap of a 6th to the tonic at the 8th fret is a country guitar cliché and is followed by an A Major triad before a D Melodic Minor idea is played, which creates a jazzy Lydian Dominant vibe. At the start of the second bar, the line briefly side-steps outside into G# Dorian before the final descending run outlines a G7b5 chord with C# (Db) on the B string.

Example 2j:

Here's another dominant line that could be used on any G7 chord. It consists of a mixture of two-note-per-string slurs and chromatics that create a Coltrane-style contour using Augmented harmony (stacking major 3rds). The figure from Example 2c is used in the second bar. A descending C Major Pentatonic run then moves towards the final target note of B.

Example 2k:

In Example 2l we explore Metheny's bluesy side. After a 1/16th-note D Minor hexatonic run, it finishes with various blues clichés delivered with smooth grace notes, slides and pull-offs, to create a slick, flowing melody.

Example 2l:

Example 2m explores a G7 Altered tonality and uses notes from the G Altered and G Phrygian Dominant scales. The motif from Example 2c is used in the first bar, and the basic pattern from Example 2b is then incorporated to create an implied G7alt to C Minor V-I cadence.

Example 2m:

The final G minor line begins with an enclosure of the root note, before a four-note descending diminished figure is shifted up chromatically five times, then the cell from Example 2b descends chromatically back to 8th position. The ending contains some slippery chromaticism that requires fast, awkward shifts to play fluently. We finish with a variation on the shell voicing idea seen earlier.

Example 2n:

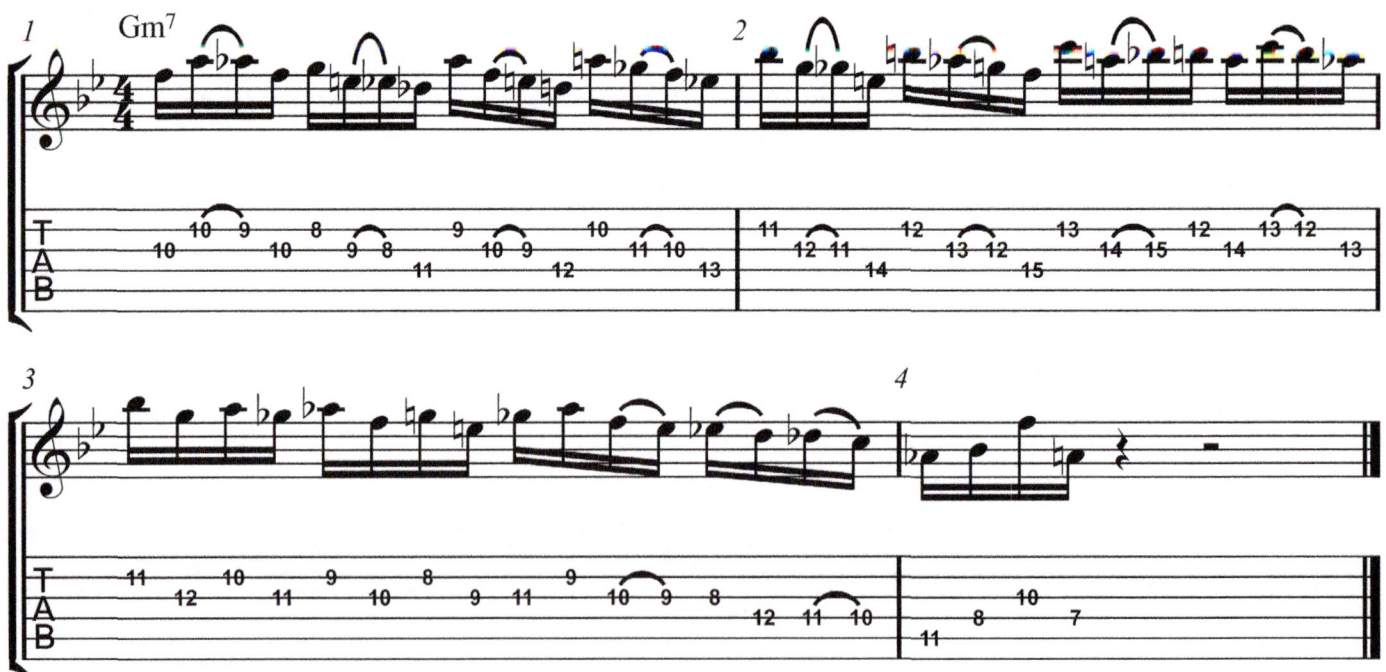

22

Chapter Three: John Scofield

John Scofield was born in 1951 in Dayton, Ohio, but grew up in Connecticut where he developed his musical interests. "Sco" is another Berklee graduate who, like his peers John Abercrombie, Mike Stern, Pat Metheny and Bill Frisell, is an outstanding composer and a master of harmony, texture and rhythm.

Scofield began his career with Billy Cobham in the mid '70s and began recording solo albums towards the end of the decade. He joined Miles Davis's band in 1982 for three albums, *Star People* (1983), *Decoy* (1984) and *You're Under Arrest* (1985). For a brief period in 1983, both Stern and Scofield were in the band together.

As the 1980s progressed, Scofield recorded a series of albums which included *Blue Matter*, *Loud Jazz* and *Electric Outlet*. These cemented his reputation and were the epitome of brash, glossy 1980s Fusion. During this time, Scofield favoured Mesa Boogie amps and used a heavily modulated, chorused sound. He has always used an Ibanez AS-200, a semi-hollow 335-style guitar.

In the '90s, Scofield signed to Blue Note and leaned more towards post-bop swing, often recording with Joe Lovano on saxophone. Towards the end of the decade, Scofield played with the organ trio Medeski, Martin and Wood, as heard on his 1998 album *A Go Go*, which dug deep into his funk roots.

Instead of using melodic cells to begin this look at John Scofield's style, we'll begin with two altered pentatonic scales which are an important part of his conceptual approach.

"Altered pentatonics" are modified pentatonic scales used to create sophisticated note choices while retaining the guitar-friendly qualities of two-note-per-string fretboard shapes.

Example 3a is a G7#9 Pentatonic scale (1 #2 3 5 b7). Since the #2 is the same note as the b3 (A# = Bb), we can view this as a standard G Minor Pentatonic scale where the 4th has been flattened to a major 3rd. This creates an ambiguous, complex, yet bluesy sound which can be used over minor, dominant or altered dominant chords.

Example 3a:

Next is a G Minor Sixth Blues Pentatonic (1 b3 b5 5 6) – an instantly Scofield-like sound. This scale is complex and sounds jazzy, bluesy and dissonant all at the same time due to its #4, which can either function as a bluesy b5 or an altered #11. The 6th (E) adds a sweet, melodic quality. While there is no major 3rd, you could still use this scale on a dominant chord to add the #9, #11 and 13, so it's incredibly versatile.

Example 3b:

Our first lick begins by ascending the G Minor Sixth Blues Pentatonic scale before merging into G Dorian. After some chromaticism on the B string there is a Schofield-esque string skip. The two-notes-per-string approach keeps the bluesy pentatonic flavour, while targeting the 9th and 13th tones adds a jazzier dynamic.

Example 3c:

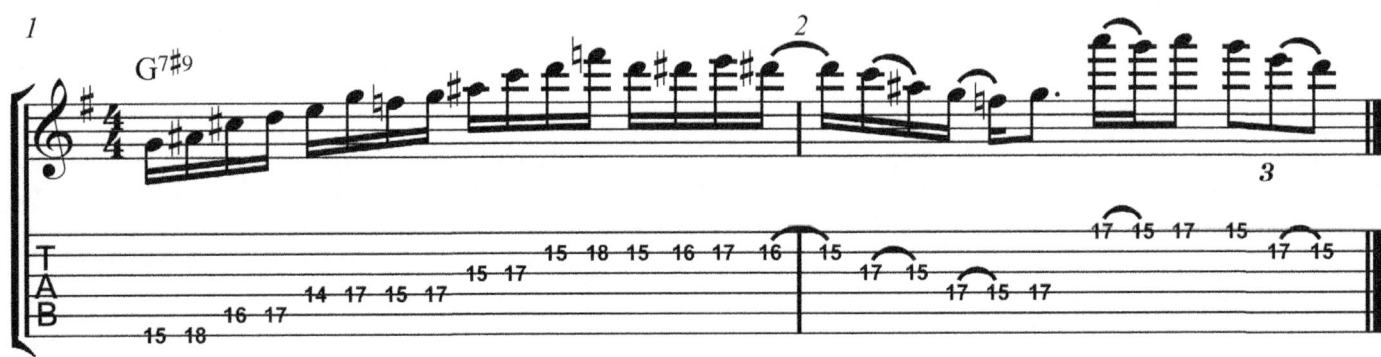

Example 3d uses G Minor Sixth Blues Pentatonic again but this time the line descends. This idea is followed by a triad figure at the end of bar two before outlining G Minor and F Major triads with an added #4. The line ends with a minor pentatonic run which side-steps into F# Minor Pentatonic before resolving back home.

Example 3d:

A diminished string skipping idea now leads us into a G Minor Pentatonic phrase. The diminished arpeggio suggests a D7b9 harmony and hints at a V-I cadence. The final part of the lick uses the G Natural Minor scale and has a descending arpeggio with stacked 4ths – another favourite device of Scofield's.

Example 3e:

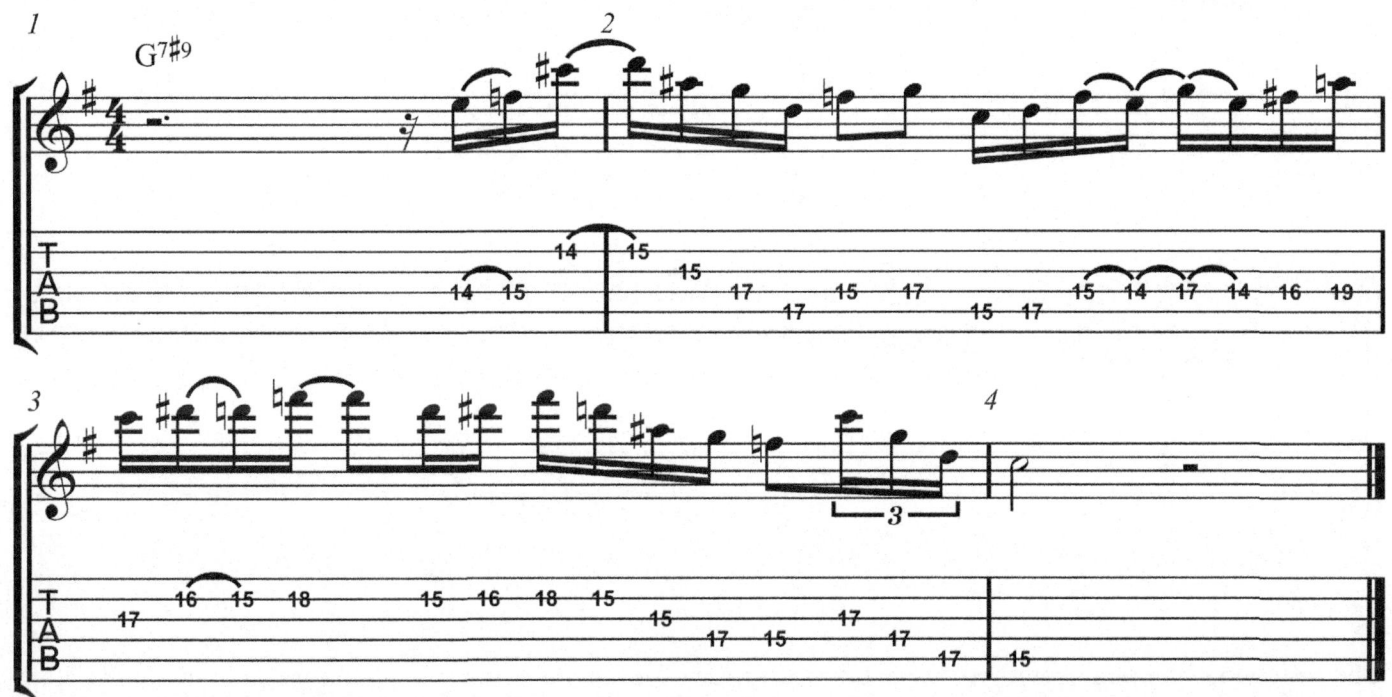

Example 3f uses the G Minor Sixth Blues Pentatonic scale with a repeated two-note motif on the B string. An E Major triad (contained in G Half-Whole Diminished) begins the descending part of the phrase at the end of bar one, before a short G Minor Pentatonic idea is followed by some side-stepping into G# Minor Pentatonic. Again, 4ths are used in both G# Minor and G Minor before finishing on a bluesy phrase.

Example 3f:

The following line begins with a bluesy minor-to-major 3rd cliché before we play a melodic idea in G Half-Whole Diminished. The descending phrase in the third bar moves through the diminished scale using a mixture of b5ths, 4ths and half step intervals.

Example 3g:

Example 3h mixes notes from G Minor Pentatonic and G Half-Whole Diminished before introducing some finger-twisting chromaticism in bar two. The line contains a nod to D Melodic Minor with a Sco-style interval skip from G to C#, before moving back to G Minor Pentatonic and concluding on the 3rd (B).

Example 3h:

The next phrase begins with another string-skipping idea using parallel minor 3rds in G Diminished. This is followed by a diminished idea that becomes an Eb Minor Pentatonic phrase (another common superimposition), before resolving to the tonic with a chromatically embellished G Minor Pentatonic line.

Example 3i:

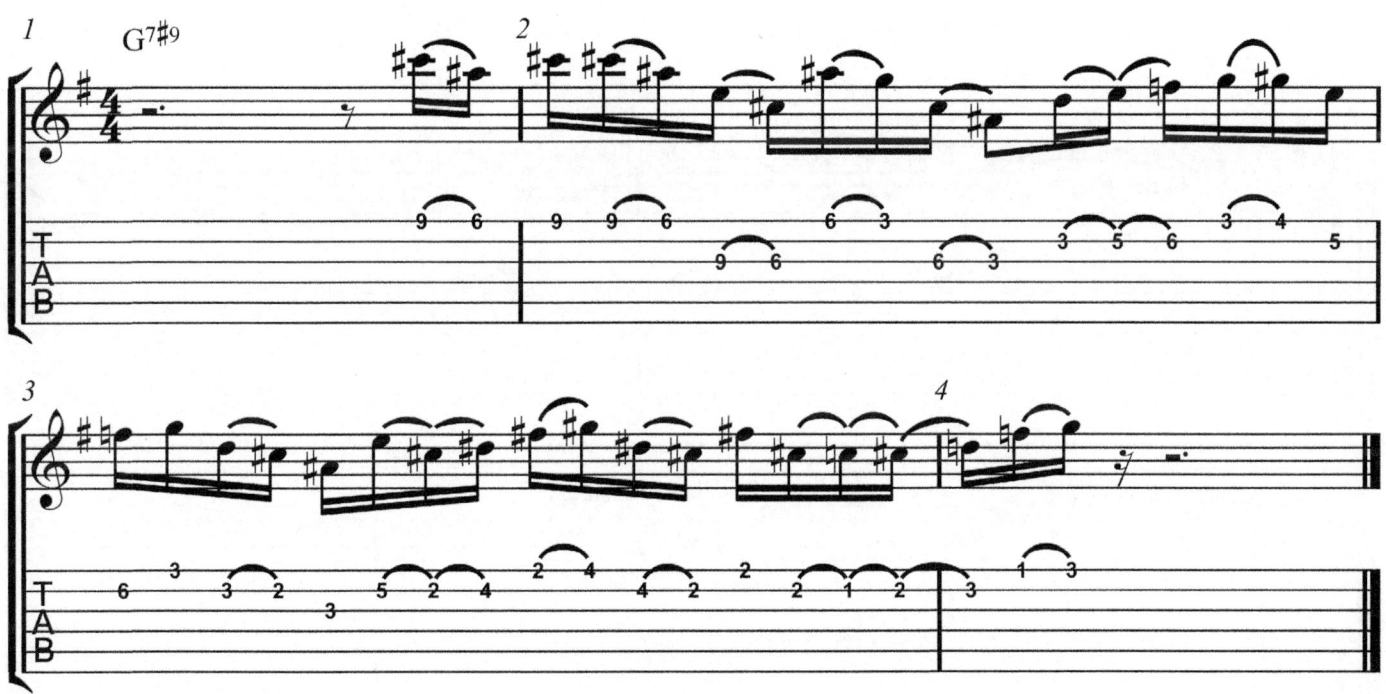

Example 3j ascends the diminished scale in a smooth, four-notes-per-string pattern, before two ascending arpeggios (G7#9 and Db Major) take us up the neck. The line ends with a dissonant descending idea which makes use of two B Augmented triads an octave apart.

Example 3j:

Next, we ascend through G7#9 Pentatonic in bar one before some finger-twisting chromaticism in bar two takes us from the b9 (Ab) to the 5th (D) on the B string. We then side-step into an F# Melodic Minor (a.k.a. F Altered scale) line with some interval skips, before we move back into G Dorian and end on the 9th (A).

Example 3k:

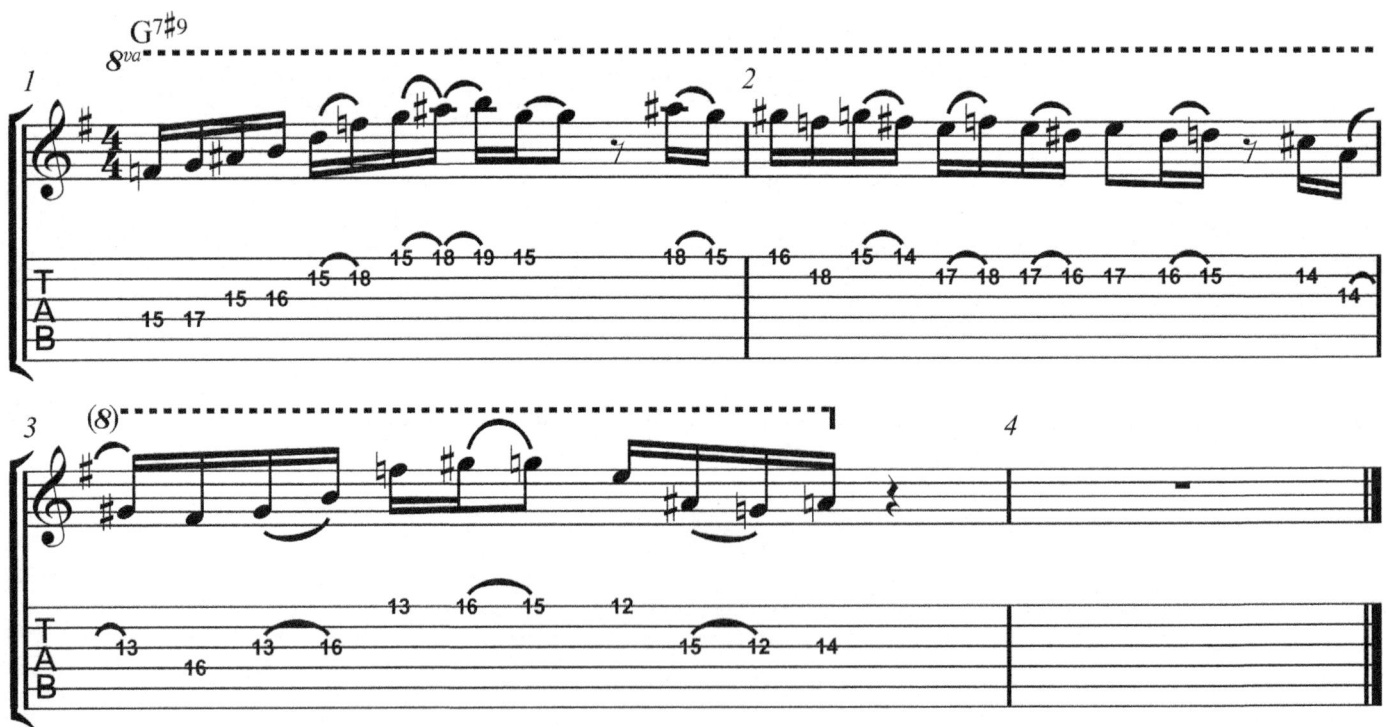

The final John Scofield idea is technically challenging and angular. It starts with an inverted major 7th figure and swaps between ascending chromaticism on the D string and descending chromaticism on the B string.

This idea is further embellished in bar three, where we end on the b7 at the 13th fret. The final bar starts with a descending phrase based on a G Diminished arpeggio. The final part is a hybrid scale that combines elements of a G Diminished arpeggio and a Gm7b5 Pentatonic scale (1 b3 4 b5 b7).

Example 3l:

Chapter Four: Robben Ford

Robben Ford was born in Woodlake, California, in 1951 and played saxophone from the age of 10 until he picked up the guitar four years later. Ford came from a musical family, and his brothers Patrick and Mark were part of a family band called The Charles Ford Blues Band, named after their father.

Ford began playing professionally with bluesmen Charlie Musselwhite and Jimmy Witherspoon at the age of 18 and quickly joined the L.A. session and Jazz Rock Fusion scene, where he played with Tom Scott. This soon led to tours with Joni Mitchell and George Harrison. For his first solo album, *The Inside Story* in 1976, Ford's backing band were the yet-to-be-formed Yellowjackets, on whose 1981 debut album he played a major role.

His popularity has continued to grow with forty years of high-quality albums as band leader. He is known for his smooth, overdriven tone and is associated with the revered Dumble amplifier – the perfect tonal mixture of grit, warmth and hi-fi clarity.

Ford started out as a Gibson 335 player before switching to a Stratocaster during a brief stint with Miles Davis in 1986. He now uses a wide range of guitars and favours Les Pauls and a 1960 Fender Telecaster. However, he also uses Gibson SGs, vintage Epiphones and PRS.

To introduce these Robben Ford-style lines we will begin with four diminished scale concepts. Although we have seen this scale earlier, we'll take a deeper dive into its structure and function.

The Half-Whole Diminished scale is an eight-note symmetrical scale formed by repeating a pattern of half-step and whole-step intervals (i.e., half-step, whole-step, half-step, whole-step etc.)

The diminished scale has always been a part of Ford's blues vocabulary, and he has explained in numerous interviews how the scale can be used as a basis for improvisation on one-chord vamps.

Although Ford's use of this scale is subtle, and he often chooses the more common blues tonalities of minor pentatonic, dorian and mixolydian, he often uses the diminished scale to create momentum and tension when moving from the I to the IV chord. He is also capable of creating powerful one-chord Fusion improvisations with this scale as the main tonality.

Example 4a teaches a useful fingering of the G Half-Whole Diminished scale that combines horizontal fingerings with vertical movement once the D string is reached.

This scale can, in theory, be used over any G Dominant chord, although you might want to exercise restraint at your next bar gig! It is especially effective over a static 7#9 vamp.

This scale run would nicely lead into the C7 chord in a I-IV-V blues if played over a G7 tonic chord.

Example 4a:

This idea demonstrates how we can move diminished scale ideas across the neck in minor 3rds. A three-note motif is moved four times before ascending through the symmetrical fingering in the previous example.

Example 4b:

Example 4c shows how Ford might descend through the diminished scale and finish with a bluesy pentatonic resolution.

Example 4c:

This idea uses some of the major triads found within the G Half-Whole Diminished scale, which contains four major and four minor triads, along with four dominant chords built on the root, 3rd, b5 and 6th degrees.

The example begins with an ascending line that outlines E Minor, E Major and Bb Major triads before ending on the major 3rd. This example gives a hint of the complexity and *polytonal* (constant ambiguous shifting of keys or tonal centres) possibilities of the Half-Whole scale.

Example 4d:

Example 4e is one of two G7 lines in this chapter. It begins with a Bm7b5 arpeggio – a common substitution built on the 3rd of the dominant chord to add a G9 extension. Descending from the root to the b7 takes us into the second bar and a position shift to the 9th fret, where the G Mixolydian Bebop scale descends into familiar blues territory.

Example 4e:

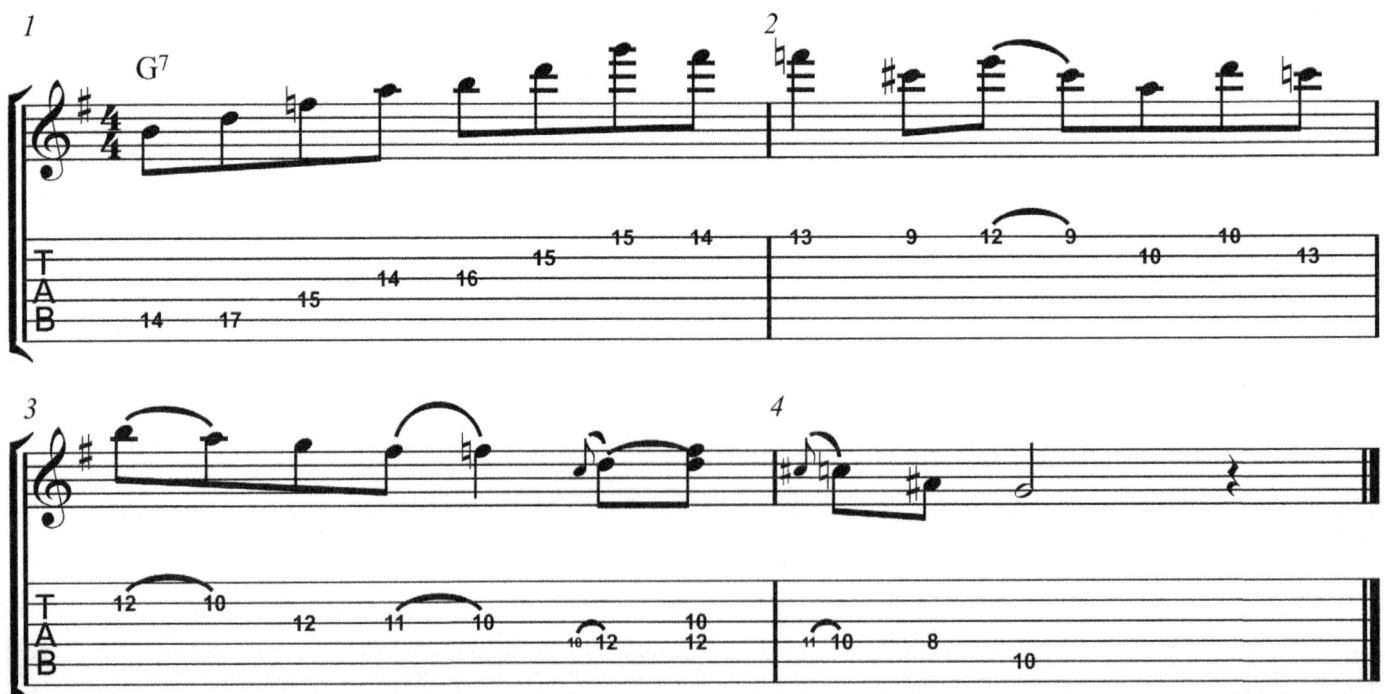

Ford often uses arpeggios and string-skips to create wide-interval sounds, and here the pull-offs create a saxophone-like flow. We shift to the 10th position to play a mixture of blues and minor scale ideas. The line ends with a blues cliché and a little b5 chromaticism.

Example 4f:

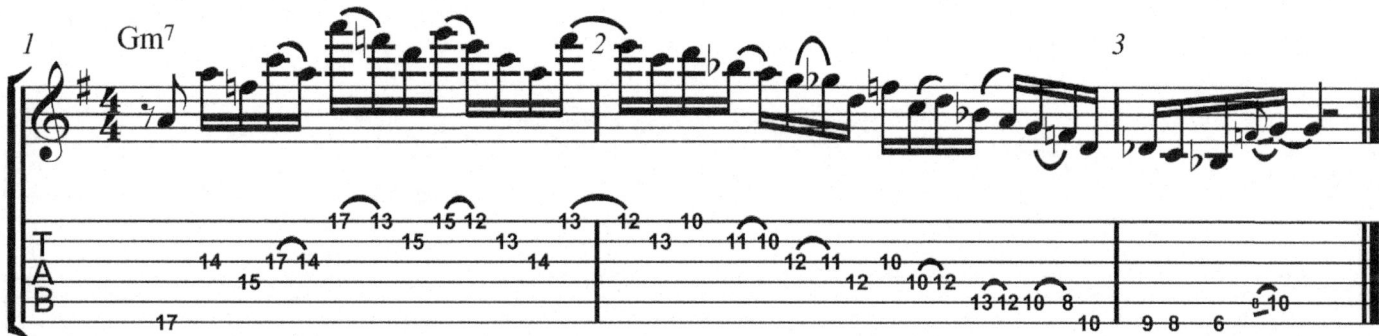

This technically challenging example is somewhat reminiscent of George Benson and represents Ford at his jazziest. The ascending arpeggios require sweeps or economy picking to be played smoothly before the line descends through G Melodic Minor using pull-offs. Bar three starts with a shift to the 10th position for an ascending hybrid blues run which ends on a classic bend.

Example 4g:

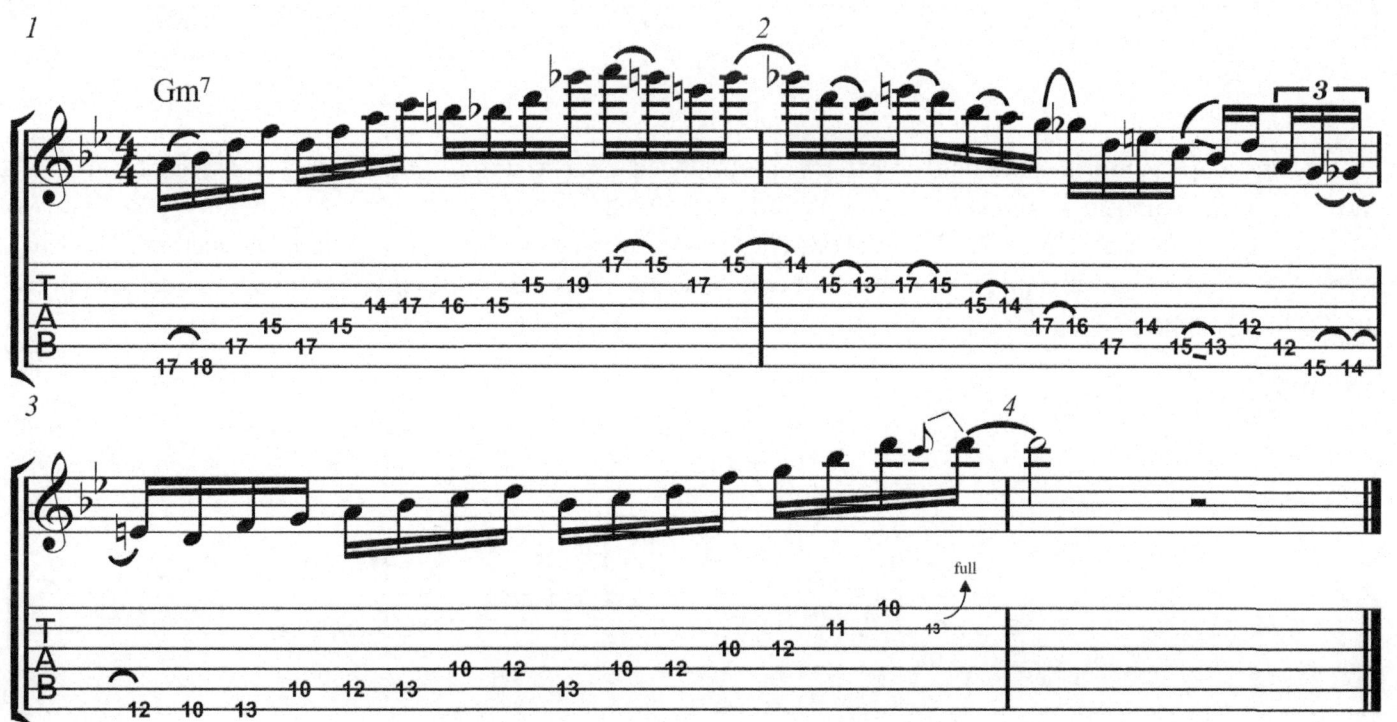

Example 4h largely sticks to G Minor Pentatonic and demonstrates how Ford uses simple scales to create Fusion-style lines. The crucial thing is not so much the note choices but the phrasing and rhythm. After two bars of dense 1/16th notes, bars three and four feature 1/8th note triplets to emphasise the contrasting bluesy feel. The final 1/16th note in bar three is immediately cut off to create a syncopated, funky effect. Again, the pull-offs are essential to create the right articulation and phrasing.

Example 4h:

In Fusion, a V7-I chord movement is often superimposed over a static chord to add a sense of harmonic movement. In Example 4i, the D7b9 is not played on the backing but is implied by the melody. The first two bars use the D Altered scale to outline a D7alt chord, then we resolve back to G Minor in bar three. This use of tension and resolution is often used to avoid one-scale-per-chord blandness. The final bar should be played aggressively, emphasising the repetition of the F note at the 18th fret.

Example 4i:

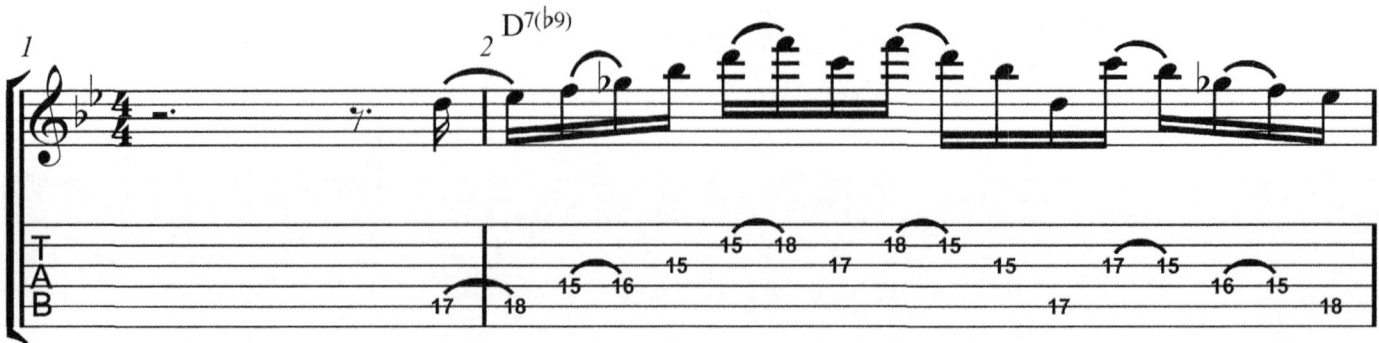

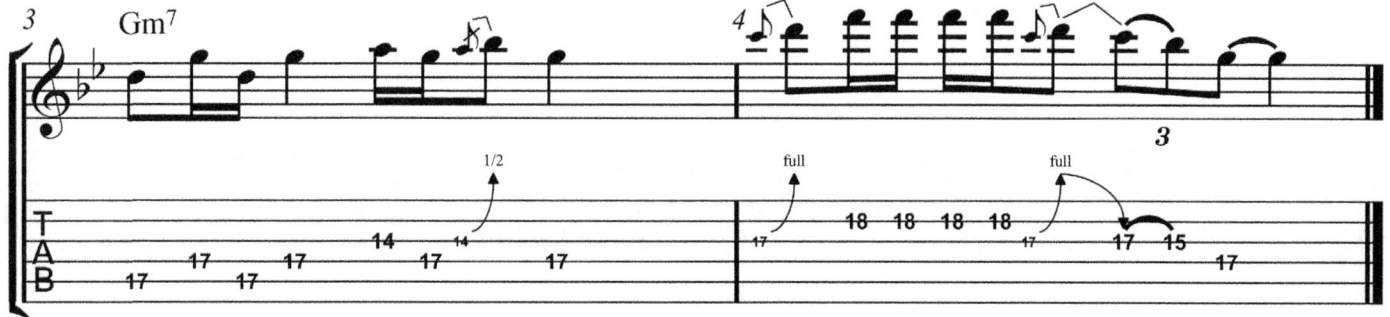

Example 4j begins by ascending G Half-Whole and emphasises the bluesy b5 interval. The final part of the line is built from a Gm(Maj7) arpeggio (1 b3 5 7) and ends with a typical blues bend from b7 to root.

Example 4j:

Varied rhythms and diminished scale triads give Example 4k a different flavour from the other lines in this chapter. Bar one starts with a laid-back blues riff, but bar two uses a combination of diminished scale runs and an E Major triad. This part of the line mixes minor and major 3rds, a common feature of both the diminished scale and the tonality of the blues. The chromaticism in bar three connects the 5th to the b3 and is an idea used by players as diverse as George Benson and Stevie Ray Vaughan.

Example 4k:

Example 4l shows how a pentatonic idea can be shifted around to create tension and surprise. A three-note motif built from G Minor Pentatonic is repeated in ascending 4ths. It then moves through F Minor and Eb Minor before returning for a pentatonic resolution.

Example 4l:

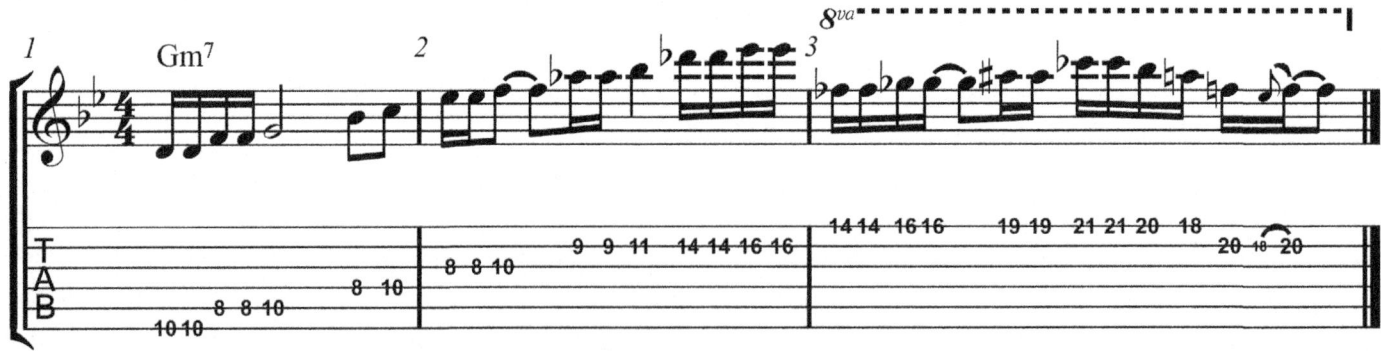

Example 4m is the second of two G7 examples. Rhythmically, the whole line is played in 1/8th note triplets, moving from G Lydian Dominant to G Minor Pentatonic via four position shifts. Notice that the F Augmented triad contains two "inside" notes (F and A) and one "outside" note (C#).

Example 4m:

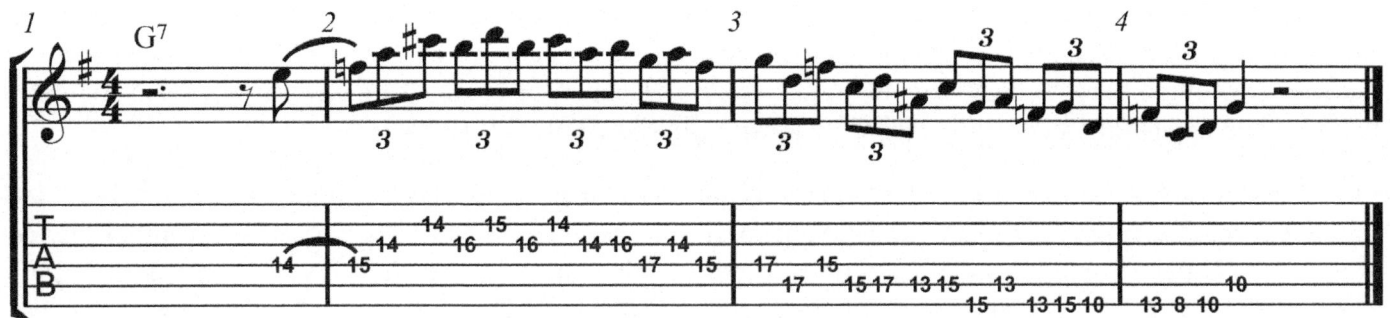

Finally, this line outlines an implied V chord at the beginning to create harmonic movement and tension. It starts with an ascending D Half-Whole idea, then a B Minor triad adds tension in the second bar before we return to more familiar G Aeolian and G Dorian territory.

Example 4n:

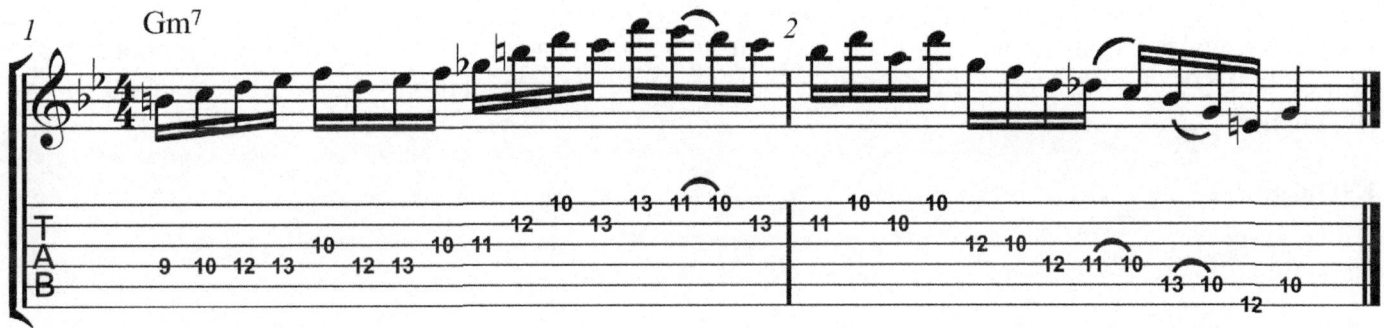

Chapter Five: Larry Carlton

Hailing from Torrance, California, Larry Carlton was born in 1948 and took up the guitar at the age of six. Carlton was playing gigs in Los Angeles in his teens and was influenced by Jazz and Blues players like Joe Pass, Wes Montgomery, B.B. King and Albert Collins. He played on the L.A. session scene in his early twenties and appeared on countless recording sessions in the 1970s and 1980s.

In addition to playing on hundreds of albums, Carlton was a member of The Crusaders from 1972-1977 and produced hits like *Put It Where You Want It*. Some of his most notable and iconic session work from this period is with Joni Mitchell on *Hejira* (1976), with Michael Jackson on *Off The Wall* (1979) and Donald Fagen on *The Nightfly* (1982). His relationship with Fagen began on the Steely Dan albums of the 1970s, especially *The Royal Scam* (1976) which contains his legendary *Kid Charlemagne* solo and outro.

It is fair to say that Carlton is one of the most expressive, dynamic players in the history of the instrument. Through his Gibson 335 and Fender Princeton and Dumble amps, his tone finds a sweet spot between clean and grit that lives just on the edge of breakup. Carlton has stated that his personal challenge is to bring B.B. King and John Coltrane together in his playing.

Our first example explores his use of superimposed arpeggios. Here we see a BbMaj7 arpeggio played over a Gm7 chord. This common substitution arises from playing a major 7 arpeggio from the b3 of a minor chord to create a minor 9th sound. (Over Gm7, the BbMaj7 arpeggio targets the b3, 5, b7 and 9).

This superimposed arpeggio is used by all Jazz musicians and is a constituent part of Wes Montgomery and Charlie Parker's playing. Notice the ascending triplet sweep and the resolution to the root after playing the 9th (A) via the b7.

Example 5a:

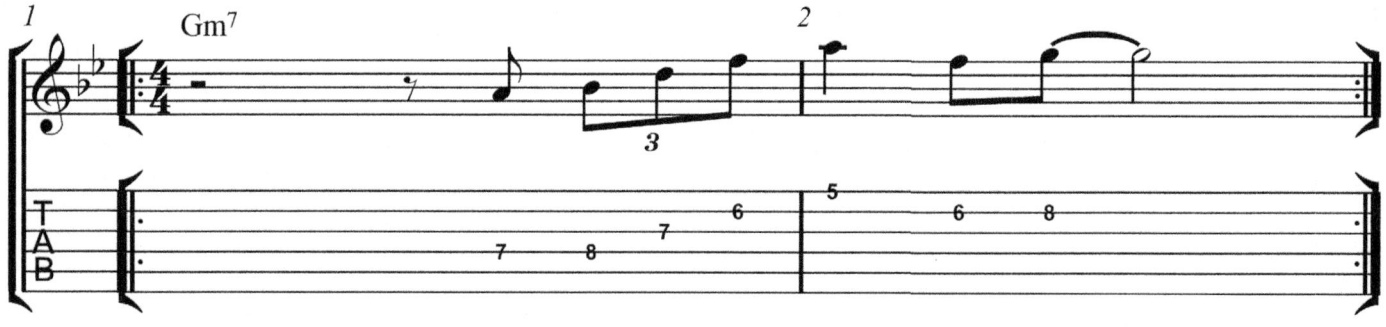

The next superimposition is to play D Minor Pentatonic over the Gm7 chord. This generates some interesting melodic possibilities as we omit the b3 (Bb) to create a more suspended or ambiguous quality. Over the Gm7 chord, D Minor Pentatonic introduces the notes D, F, G, A and C. Reordered with a root note of G, these intervals are 1, 9, 11, 5 and b7.

Notice the repeated A note and how the pull-offs are displaced so that they do not fall predictably.

Example 5b:

The next idea shows how Carlton uses major triads from the Half-Whole Diminished scale over Dominant chords. Here we have G, Bb, E and C# Major triads played in different inversions. The line could work over a static G7 altered vamp or as part of a V7-I in the key of C.

Example 5c:

This line also uses superimposed arpeggios and shows how you can move smoothly from extended harmony to convincing blues phrases. Carlton's articulation is completely authentic and the use of the major 7 (F#) adds tension to the Gm7 chord which is resolved with the blues lick. You can choose to leap to the 13th fret bend or slide (*glissando*) into it.

Example 5d:

Example 5e is a creative use of descending 4ths using G Minor Pentatonic. We outline a BbMaj7 arpeggio in bar three, shifting from the triplet rhythm to 1/16th notes to increase momentum. The end of the phrase highlights the major 6th (E) to emphasise the Dorian flavour. The hammer-ons and pull-offs are essential for fluency.

Example 5e:

This short lick shows one way in which Carlton uses triad pairs over Dominant 7 chords. Here, over the G7 chord, he weaves between two diatonic triads of G Major and F Major which use six of the seven notes of the mode. By using these "stacked" structures soloists can create more angular lines.

One of the most interesting aspects of this example is the wide interval leap from F to C on the 8th fret. This C creates a suspended 4th sound before the phrase moves back to the 3rd at the 7th fret, then descends using another inversion of the G Major triad.

Example 5f:

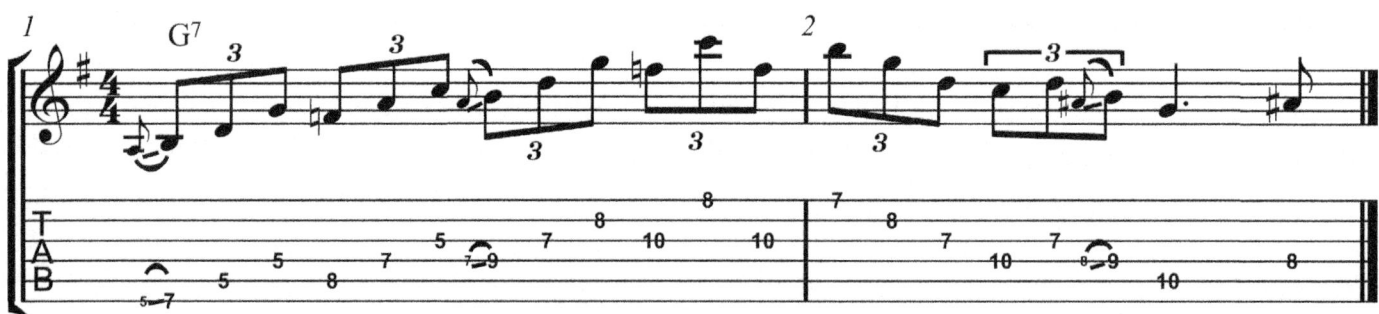

Example 5g starts with a two-octave Dm9 arpeggio. The high C on the final 1/16th note of bar one signals a transition to A Minor Pentatonic, which superimposes the root, 4th, 5th, 6th and 9th. The lack of a b3 in this scale choice creates an ambiguous tonality.

Example 5g:

Example 5h combines G Minor and D Minor Pentatonic in different rhythmic groupings to create some atypical blues ideas. The ascending triplet figures use G Major Hybrid Blues ideas and land in the "B.B. Box".

Example 5h:

Here, Carlton uses A Minor Pentatonic pedal tone ideas to add the root, 2nd, 4th, 5th and 6th to the G7 chord that underpins the harmony. The ascending triplet triad pairs are reminiscent of previous examples but played in a higher octave. The end returns to the pedal-tone idea but now uses the root as the pedal while descending through G Minor Pentatonic and G Mixolydian.

Example 5i:

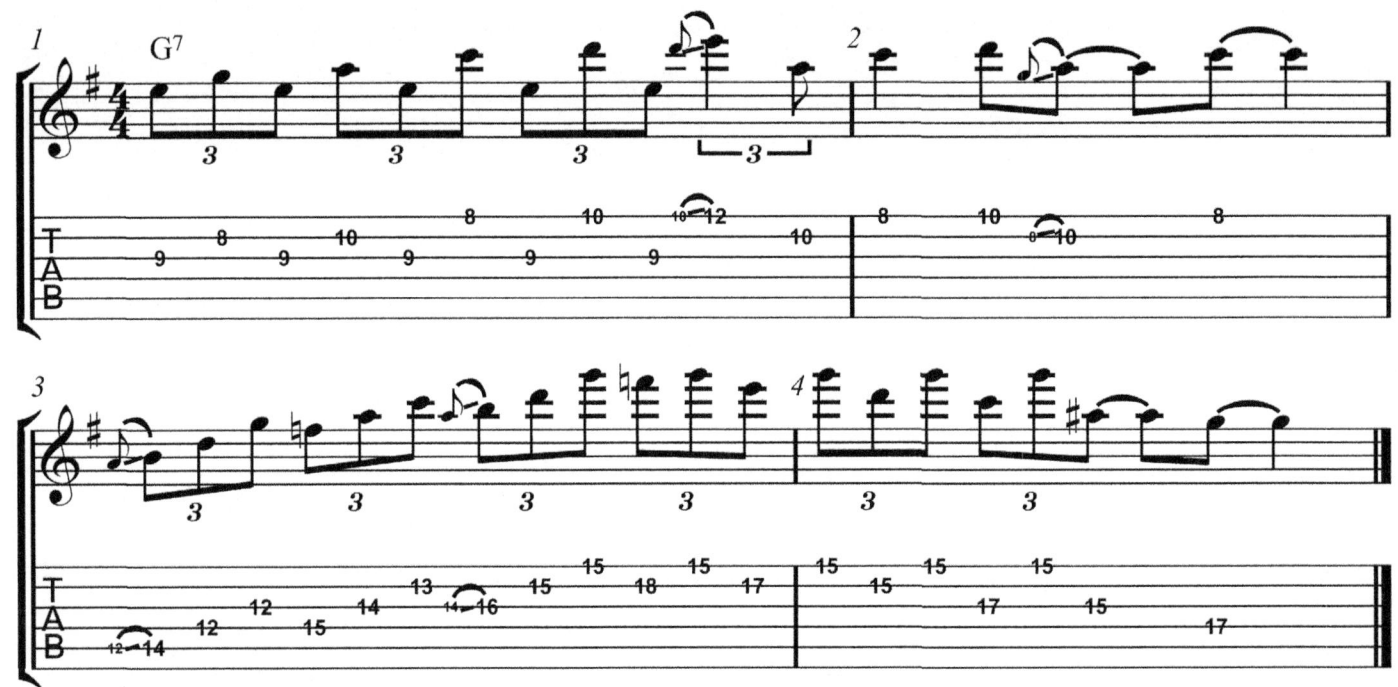

Example 5j begins with familiar blues/pentatonic phrases then ascends a Dm7 arpeggio before moving back to G Minor Pentatonic. This line then moves to A Minor, followed by a *glissando* to the 17th fret. This is followed by a superimposed BbMaj7 arpeggio which descends to the 4th.

Example 5j:

Here, a BbMaj7 arpeggio is played over Gm7 but a string-skip adds interest to the first bar. The open string at the end of bar one transitions into A Minor Pentatonic which is superimposed over Gm7. This line shows how even familiar material can take on new life when used in a less obvious environment.

Example 5k:

Example 5l ascends using G Aeolian combined with BbMaj7 and EbMaj7 arpeggios. After a repeated high D, the line descends the D Minor Blues scale with interval leaps and direction changes. The final bend at the 13th fret is approached with a slide, which works best starting from the 10th fret.

Example 5l:

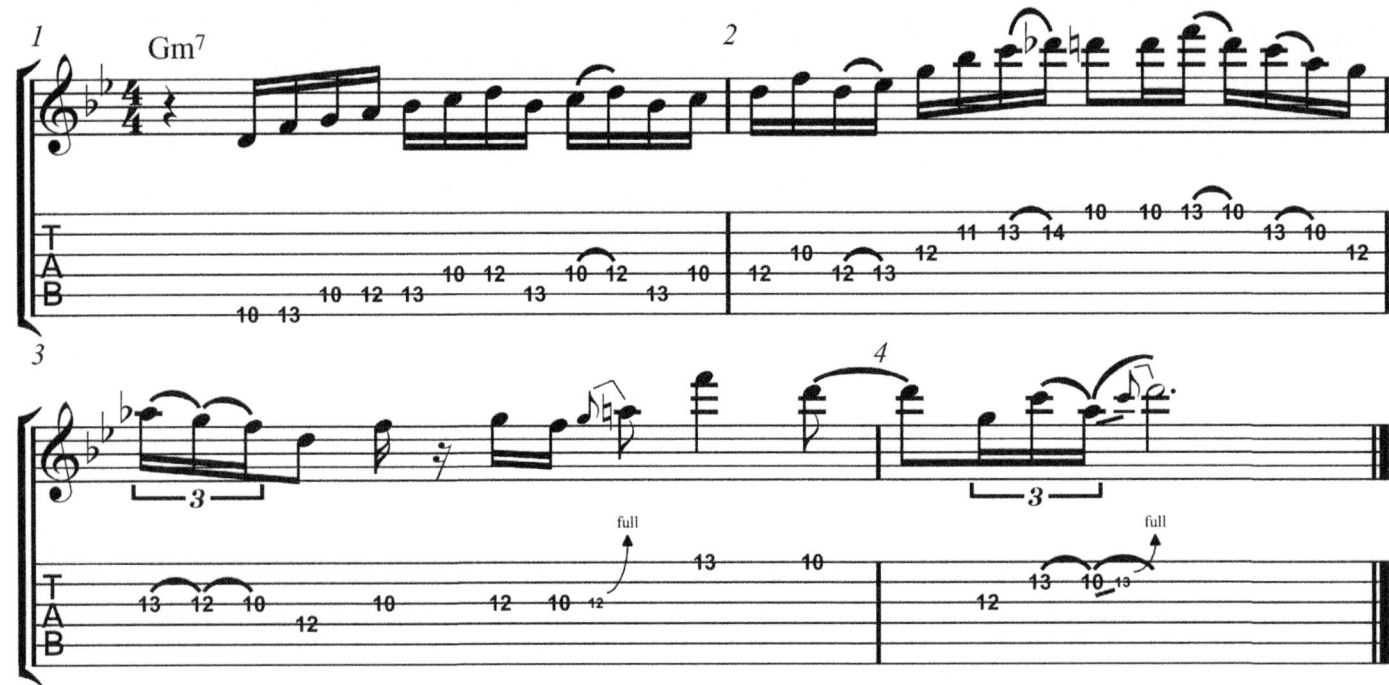

Example 5m stacks pentatonic 4ths in ascending groups of three. Use a down-down-up picking pattern to aid fluent articulation of these groupings. The original motif is repeated twice before we again use a BbMaj7 arpeggio to create a minor 9 sound over Gm7.

Example 5m:

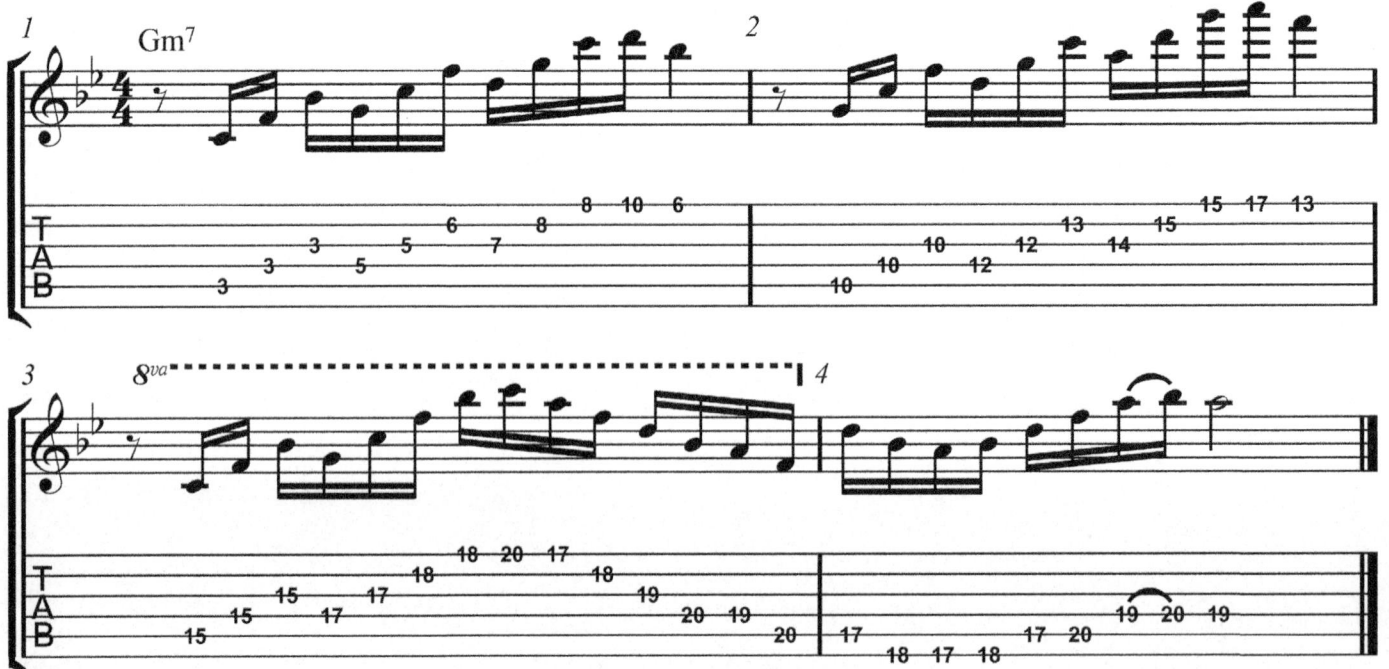

This final D Harmonic Minor idea implies a Dorian #4 tonality over Gm7 in a broken triplet pattern, which Carlton uses to break up predictable scales. The final part of the line switches to G Harmonic Minor, ending with a tense 7th to create a Gm(Maj7) texture.

Example 5n:

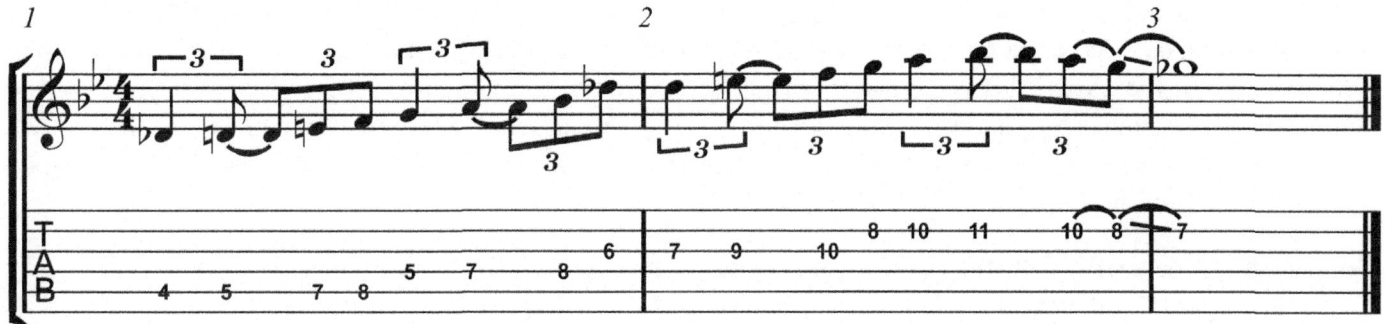

Chapter Six: Allan Holdsworth

Allan Holdsworth was born on August 6th, 1948, in Manningham, England. His father, Sam, was a Jazz pianist and his collection of Jazz records helped influenced Holdsworth's first musical steps. He advanced quickly on the guitar and by the mid-1960s was touring both England and Germany in local Beatles-style groups such as The Crusaders, and Mick Judge and His Jurymen.

Dissatisfied that only dance hall gigs were available to professional guitarists, and unhappy with the commercial arrangements of the day, Holdsworth sought out different vehicles for his evolving Fusion style. This led to stints with bands such as Igginbottom, Sunship and Nucleus. He quickly emerged as a mainstay of the English progressive Rock scene in the early 1970s, and a brief period with the Cream-inspired band Tempest helped further his reputation.

Tempest fitted perfectly with the growing pantheon of progressive Rock bands which included Yes, King Crimson, Genesis and Pink Floyd. Other bands sought out Holdsworth's virtuosity and stints with Soft Machine and Gong allowed him to further explore his vision of the guitar's expressive potential. A tour with Yes drummer Bill Bruford's band followed, and the band "U.K." grew out of this relationship.

Holdsworth began his solo career at the end of the '70s, and a series of boundary-pushing albums featuring his unique compositions and dazzling chops followed.

He continued to release innovative Fusion albums in the mid-1980s, evolving both his fretboard mastery and tone. These albums included *IOU*, *Road Games*, *Metal Fatigue* and *Sand*, all released in a creative run between 1982 and 1987. The albums he recorded in the second part of his solo career, starting with *Secrets* in 1989 and culminating in *The Sixteen Men of Tain* in 2000, helped to cement Fusion as a fully-fledged genre.

Holdsworth's death in 2017 was a shock to the guitar community and wider musical world. Following his death, respect and admiration for his music has been found by new audiences.

Holdsworth's Technique

Holdsworth's style is so highly evolved that it defies reduction into "signature licks". However, as with the other players covered in this book, there are some recognisable motifs, melodic cells, and stylistic traits that we might extract or identify as "Holdsworthian".

We must acknowledge Holdsworth's mastery of legato, and a strong legato technique is required to play the following lines cleanly. It is outside the scope of this book to go into a detailed analysis of legato technique, but Chris Brooks' book, *Legato Guitar Technique Mastery* is an excellent place to start.

Creating an identical articulation, whether a note is picked or played with legato, is the highest priority in this style. A "square-on" hand and fingering position, with the thumb placed on the middle of the back of the neck and pointing upwards to form a 90-degree angle to the neck, allows the greatest reach for the fingers.

Example 6a contains two three-note motifs that Holdsworth used in different harmonic settings. It is most straightforward to see them as two fragments derived from the diminished scale. The first structure consists of root, b3 and 3rd, and the second of root, b2 and 3rd. These fragments can be moved around individually or combined, often in b5 or major 3rd intervals, as shown in the example.

Example 6a:

Here's an approach Holdsworth used to embellish target notes with an enclosure. This idea targets the 5th of Gm7 (D) and can be seen as his version of the classic "half-step below/chord tone above" embellishment of a target note. Here, however, he uses four notes to enclose the target D note.

Example 6b:

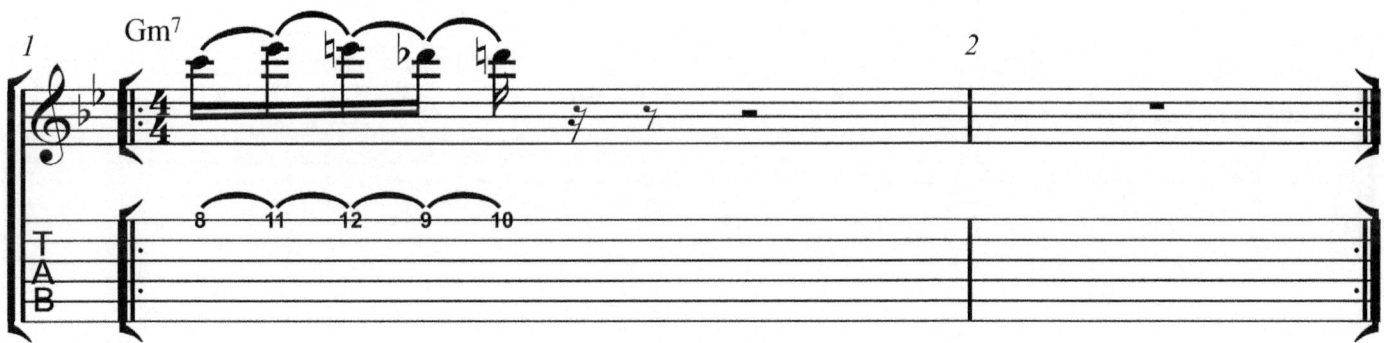

The next fragments hint at Holdsworth's use of *polytonality* (two or more tonalities played simultaneously or alternately) to create harmonic density over a root note. Here, the key centre is G Minor, and we start with a three-note D Minor Pentatonic idea. The example then uses the three-note motif from Example 6a, built from an Eb, played descending.

Example 6c:

The final motif takes the first structure from Example 6a, plays it in quintuplets, and moves in b5 intervals. The texture here is definitely Holdsworthian and should suggest to the ears a world of possibilities.

Example 6d:

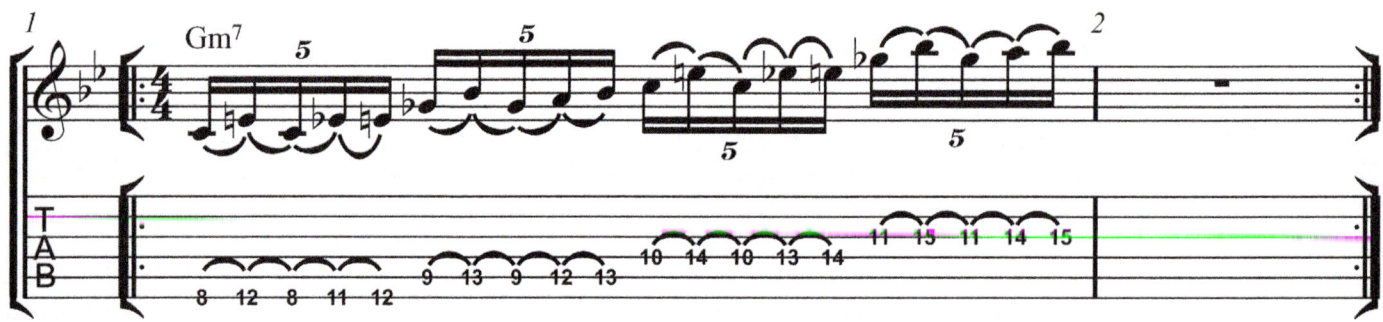

Next, we begin with a line that moves through all twelve keys using a "root-3rd-2nd-root" idea beginning in C Major. The concept is that, as the fingers ascend the fretboard, the line descends through all 12 keys in half steps, one-by-one.

Harmonically, this amounts to an extended exercise in tension and release as we pass through every key. Some of these three-note groupings have all three notes in common with the underlying G Dorian and other groupings have none.

Example 6e:

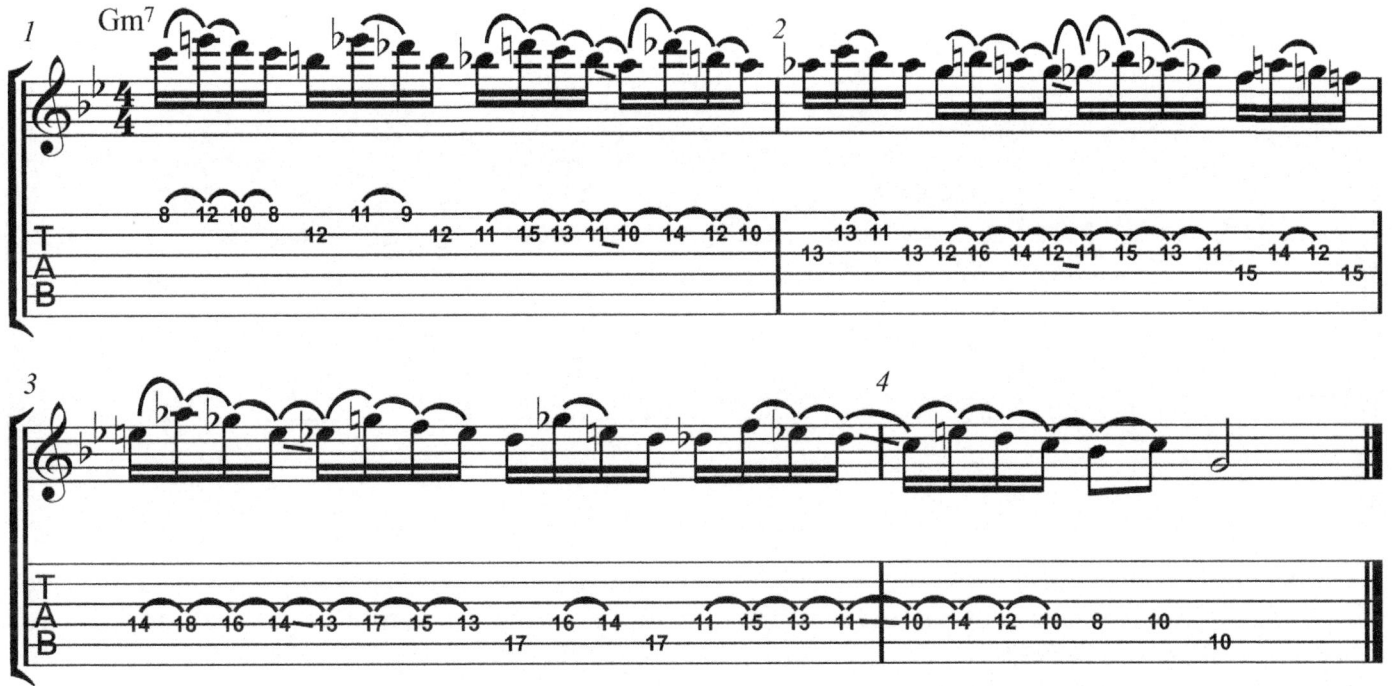

On the third beat of bar two, the line switches to using the enclosure motif from Example 6b to target a Bb, the 3rd of the Gm7 chord. The example then continues to use this approach in the third bar to target the other notes of the G Minor triad, (D and G). The lick ends with a simple, melodic G Minor idea.

Example 6f:

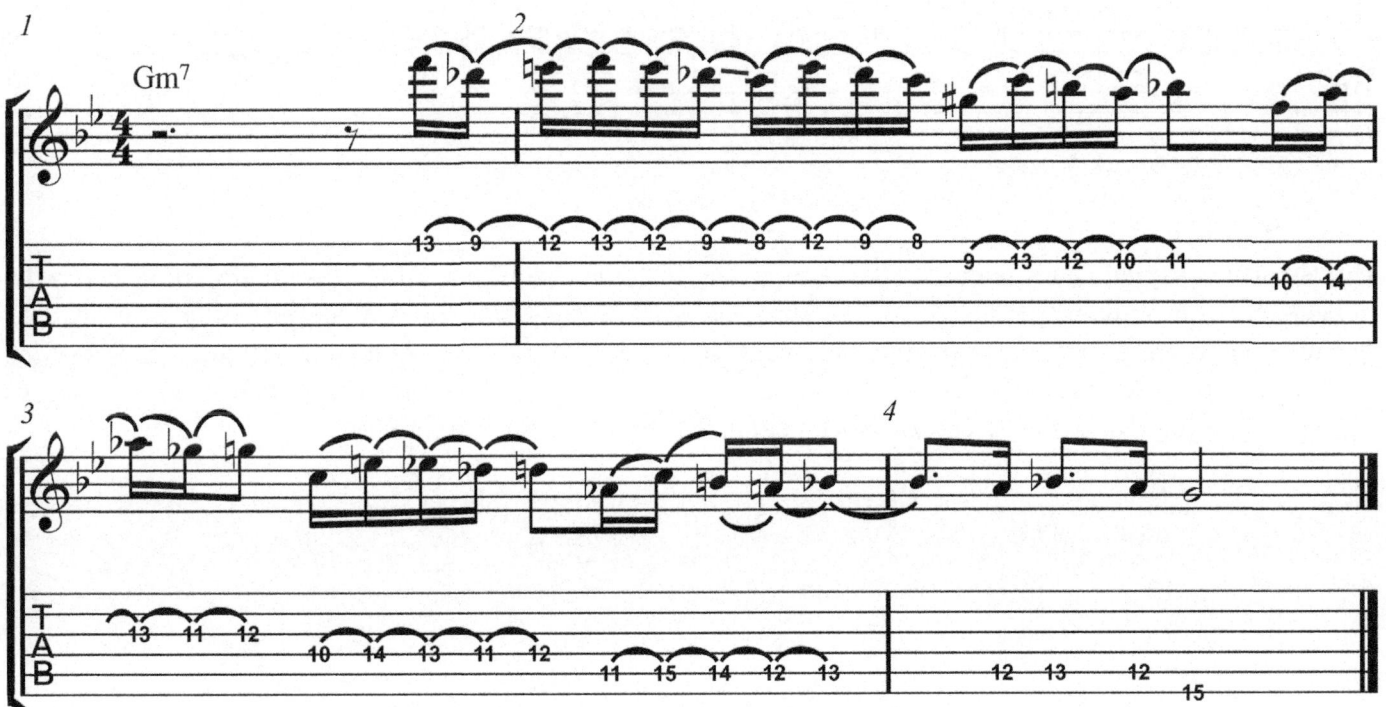

Now we begin with an enclosure of the b6 before a five-note chromatic enclosure is played five times to target the the 9th and b6 alternately.

Example 6g:

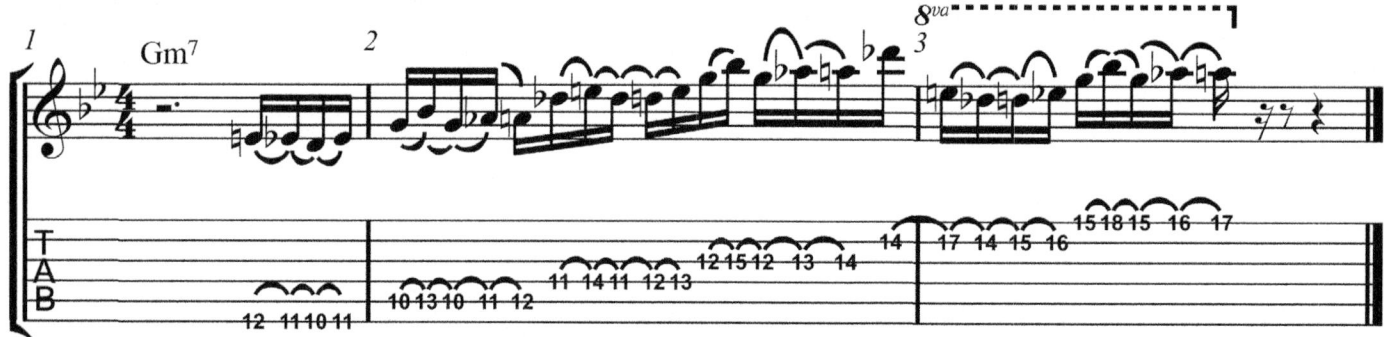

Example 6h starts by using a familiar pentatonic idea but quickly takes a turn into some extreme dissonance by using both the G Whole-Half and G Half-Whole scales (and even a fragment of G Whole Tone) before resolving to G Dorian in bar two.

Example 6h:

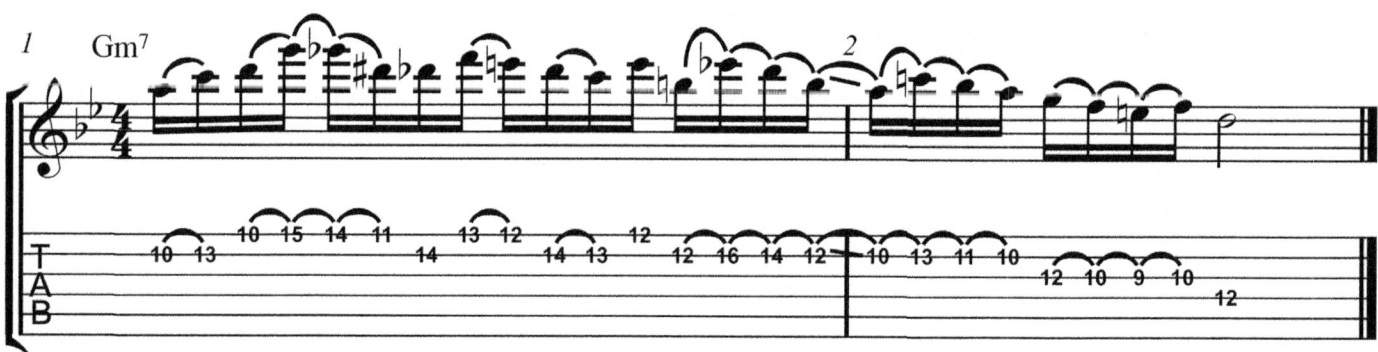

Holdsworth's playing can be surprisingly diatonic and melodic at times, a side of his playing reflected in the next example. In some ways, this is a typical three-note-per-string G Dorian idea, not dissimilar to how Rock or Metal players might use the scale. Points of interest, however, are the C note doubled on the 17th fret of the G string and the 13th fret of the B string. Some unusual rhythmic interest is added via the five-note groupings played in 1/16th notes, which create displacement and a sense of disorientation

Example 6i:

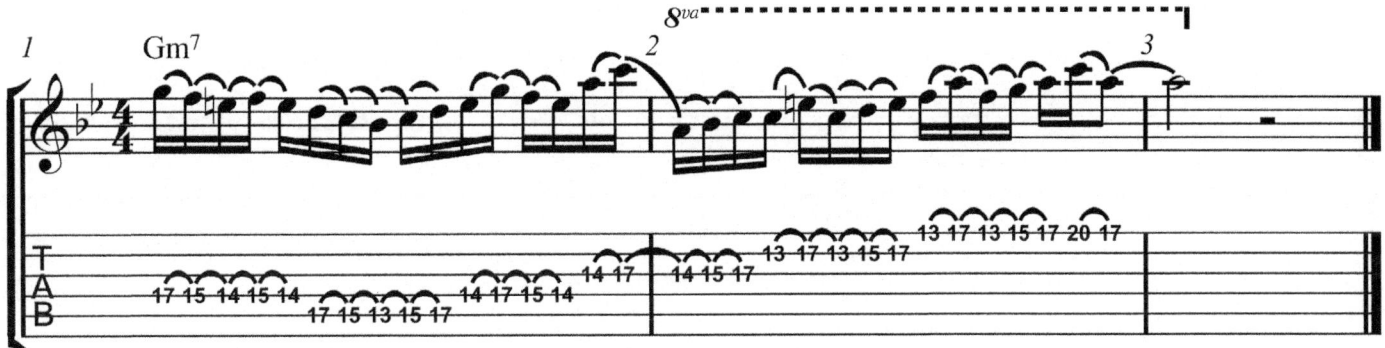

Example 6j takes the second melodic cell from Example 6a (root, b2 and 3rd) and moves it around in parallel. I.e., the first note changes and the other two retain the same intervallic relationship with it. The same note is played on different strings for an overlapping or doubling effect. This saxophone-like sound is one that Holdsworth strived for and is known by saxophonists as "false fingering". The lowest note of each three-note grouping (A, F and C#) spells out an augmented chord.

Example 6j:

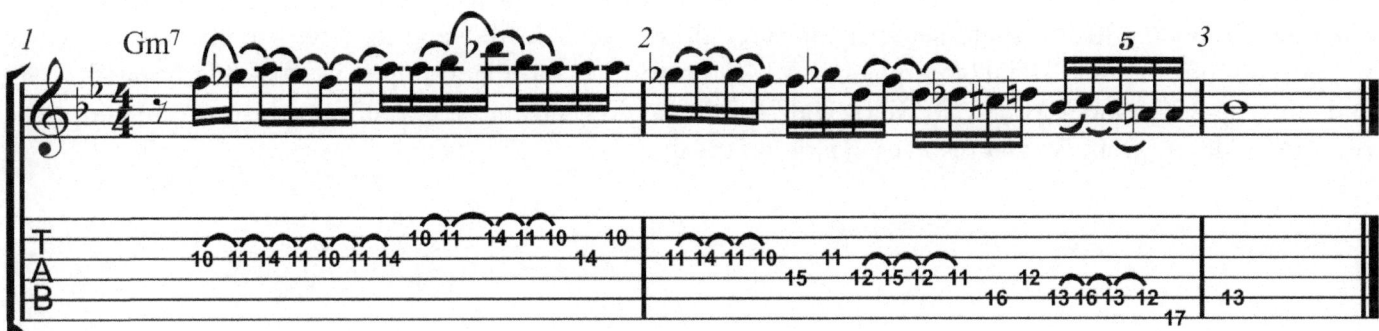

Example 6k takes the same root, b2, 3rd cell but now ascends. It is played twice on each string with a gap of a half-step between each iteration. Again, the first note of each eight-note grouping is a major 3rd away from the preceding one and creates an augmented sound. From another perspective, the line contains all twelve tones organised in four augmented triads (Ab, A, Bb, B) played using one three-note cell.

Example 6k:

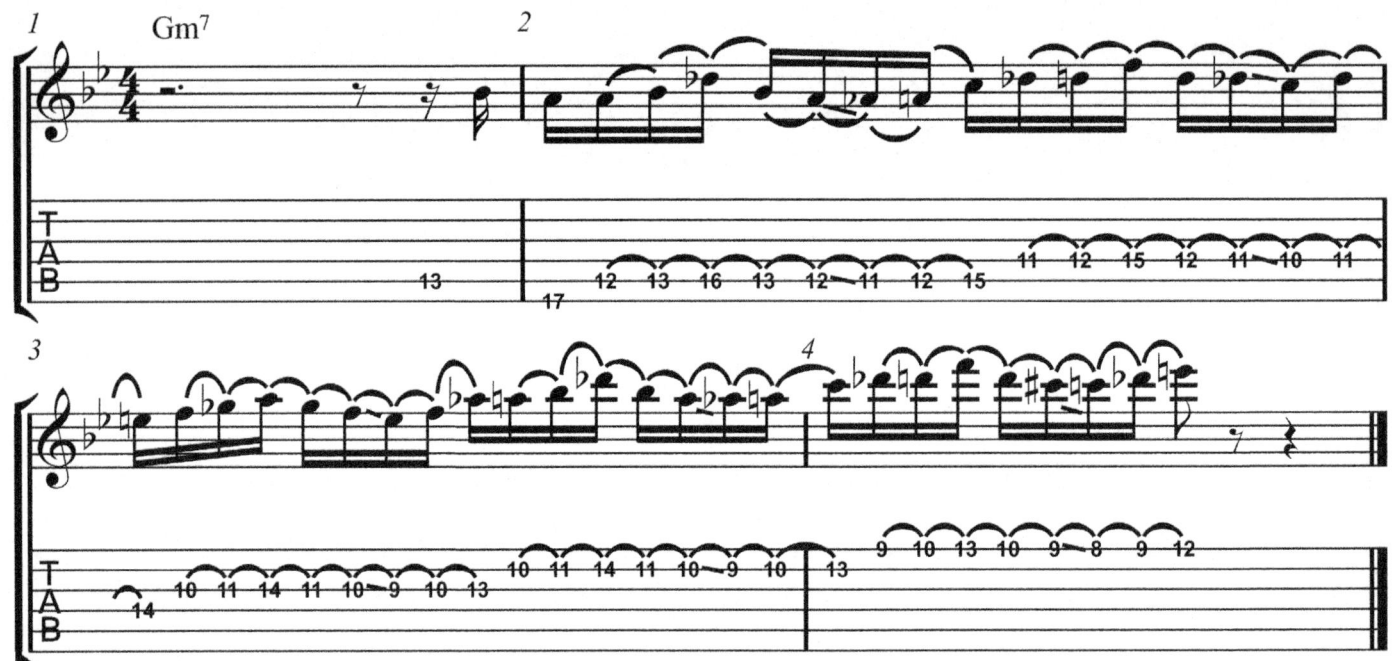

Example 6l takes a Major7#5 based arpeggio pattern and moves it in ascending Major 3rds, creating an Augmented sound. This two-note-per-string idea requires a lot of shifting and stretching to play cleanly. Once the line reaches the final Dmaj7#5 arpeggio in 14th position, a chromatic fragment descends from Bb to F# and suggests G Melodic Minor. B Minor and Db7 arpeggios end the lick, with a reprise of the chromatic descending figure from Bb that resolves clearly on the tonic.

Example 6l:

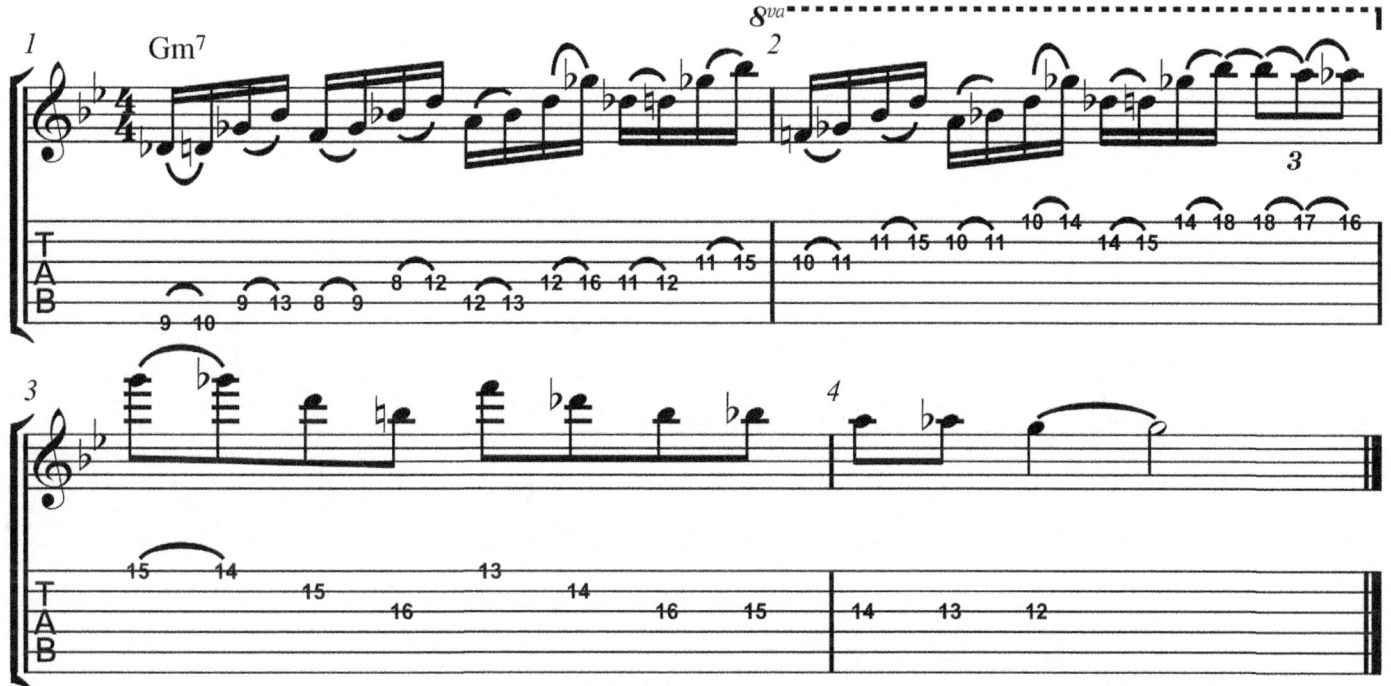

This next line combines major 7#5 and major 7 arpeggios in an eight-note idea that could also be seen as combining examples 6a and 6b. Here we flip the "descending while ascending" idea as the lick ascends in pitch while descending the fretboard. Use fingers 1 then 2 for the first two notes, then 1-4-3-1-1-2. Slide between any two notes played consecutively with the first finger. The final bar is a descending G Melodic Minor idea with a strong emphasis on the Bb Augmented triads found within the scale.

Example 6m:

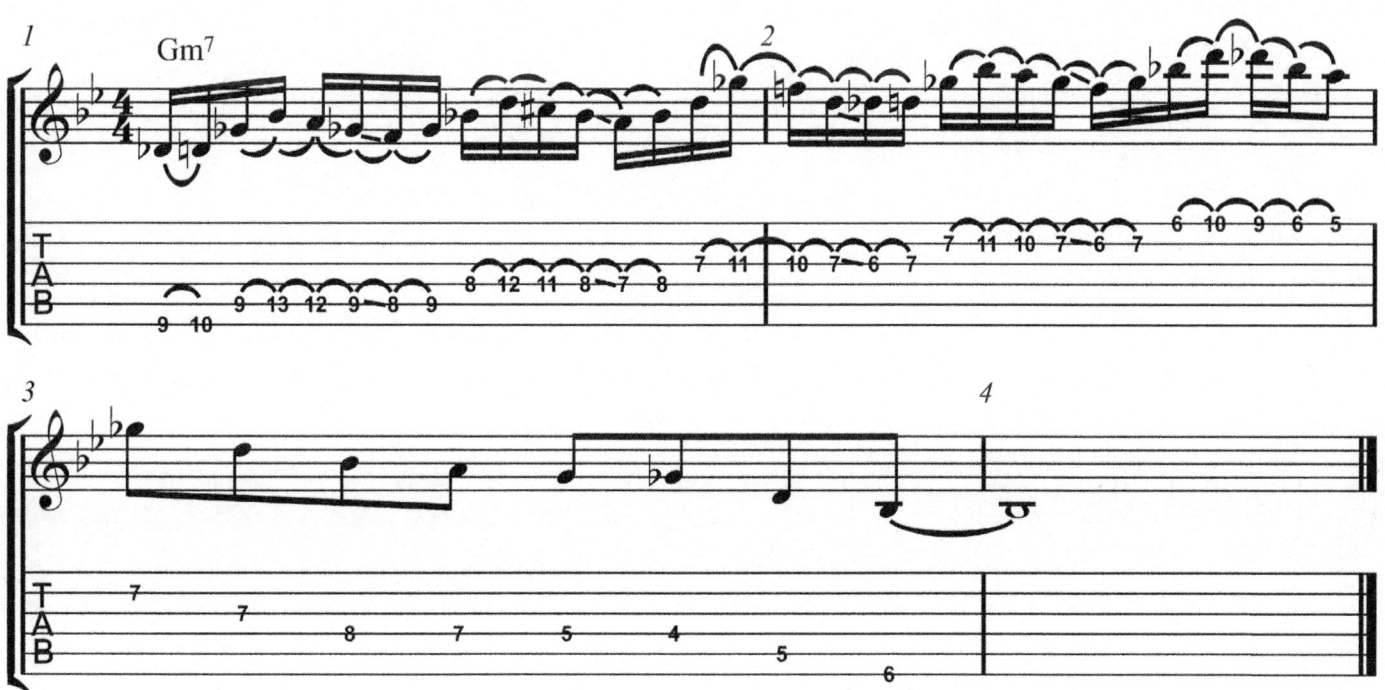

Example 6n uses G Melodic Minor in a thirteen-note pattern that displaces due to being played in 1/16th notes. After the first three notes of each thirteen-note section, shift up two frets, then one fret when you change strings. The first eight notes of each section come from a five-note Whole Tone fragment taken from the G Melodic Minor scale. The line ends with a string-skip into straightforward triplet figures.

Example 6n:

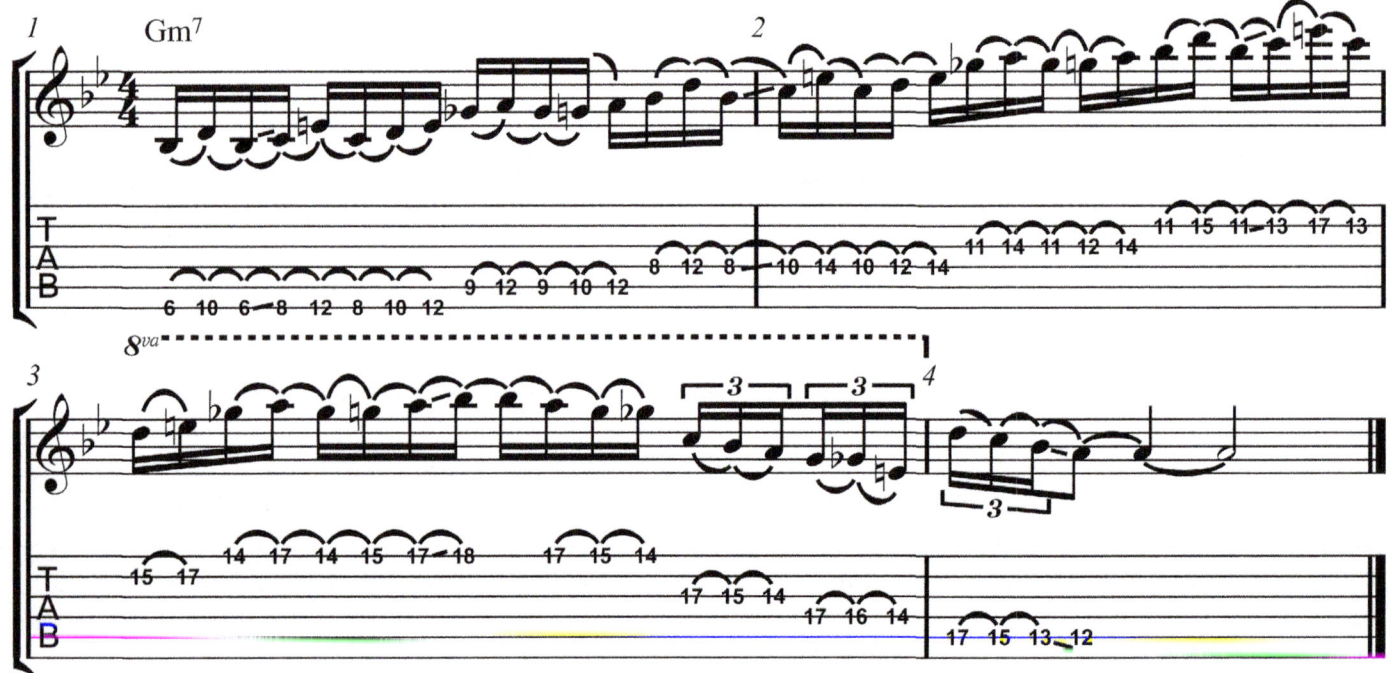

Chapter Seven: John McLaughlin

John McLaughlin was born in Doncaster, Yorkshire, on January 4th, 1942, and it's fair to say that he is the "Godfather" of Jazz-Rock Fusion guitar. His first steps in music were taken on the piano and violin but he started to learn guitar at age 11. His early influences included Django Reinhardt, Tal Farlow and, most significantly, John Coltrane.

McLaughlin moved to London in the early 1960s and found work in studios and with bands in London's growing Blues/RnB scene. He worked as a sideman for bandleaders Alexis Korner and Graham Bond, honing his craft and developing his musical vision before recording his debut album, *Extrapolation* in 1969.

These early experiments in post-bop Jazz came to the attention of Tony Williams and Miles Davis, who recruited McLaughlin for the ground-breaking Fusion albums *In a Silent Way* (1969) and *Bitches Brew* (1970).

McLaughlin's ferocious single note lines on *Bitches Brew* led the way for Fusion guitar, while his reputation was cemented in *The Mahavishnu Orchestra*, where his vision took flight in collaboration with Billy Cobham and Jan Hammer. The albums *Inner Mounting Flame* (1971) and *Birds of Fire* (1972) announced that guitar-based Fusion had arrived, with their powerful blend of complex time signatures, mixed modality, exotic scales and Eastern-sounding riffs.

McLaughlin's style continued to grow and evolve with Shakti, which explored his Eastern influences and later with The Guitar Trio, where he expanded the European guitar traditions of Flamenco, Gypsy and Folk into something fresh. In the '90s he recorded a series of albums that showcased his compositional skill, musicality and technique. The albums *Tokyo Live*, *After the Rain*, *The Promise* and *The Heart of Things* reaffirmed his electric Jazz guitar roots.

We will begin by looking at certain idiomatic aspects of McLaughlin's approach before combining them into more musical ideas.

Example 7a breaks the diminished scale into a series of four-note cells called *tetrachords* – an idea that McLaughlin took from John Coltrane. These cells have the formula root, 2nd, 3rd, 5th and the first fragment consists of these four-note cells daisy chained together. The tetrachord approach can be applied to other scales if you want to incorporate some McLaughlin traits into your playing.

Example 7a:

Example 7b demonstrates the kind of diminished run that McLaughlin might play horizontally across the fretboard. Here, focus on strong alternate picking, as these types of lines gave birth to shred guitar and are now a common fixture in Rock and Metal.

Example 7b:

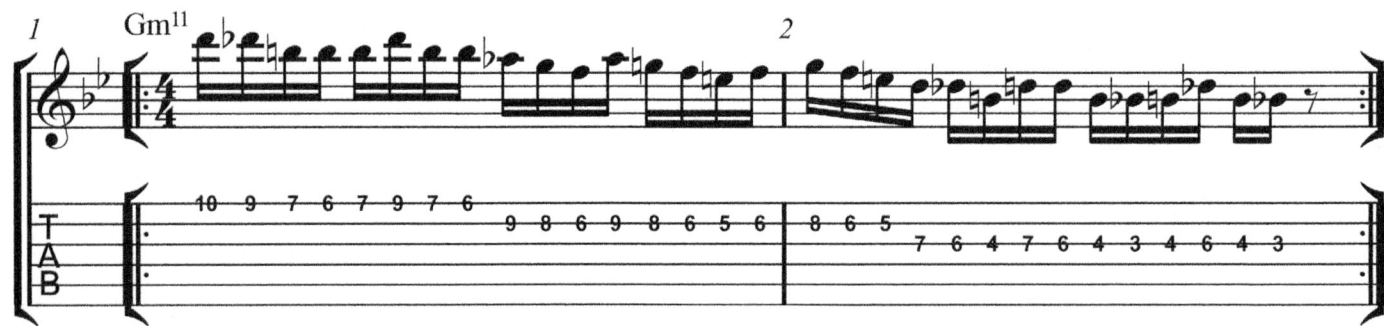

Example 7c uses a mixture of rhythmic groupings to create an exotic, vortex-like effect on a descending sequence. The mixture of four- and five-note groupings is not as difficult as it might first appear and should flow smoothly after some practice.

Example 7c:

Our first line uses the major triads found within the G Half-Whole scale in the first bar before moving to an A7 based arpeggio played over a G Minor tonality to create an outside quality. The final part concludes with fragments of C and Eb Melodic Minor.

Example 7d:

Example 7e is based around Whole Tone and Augmented fragments, and highlights McLaughlin's ever-shifting harmonic ideas with an audacious use of chromaticism that defies "traditional" harmonic explanation. There are suggestions of D Melodic Minor in the first bar and A Melodic Minor in the second, suggesting G7 and D7 over the underlying G Minor tonality. The final bar uses C Whole Tone which connects with the G Minor tonality due to the presence of the b3.

Example 7e:

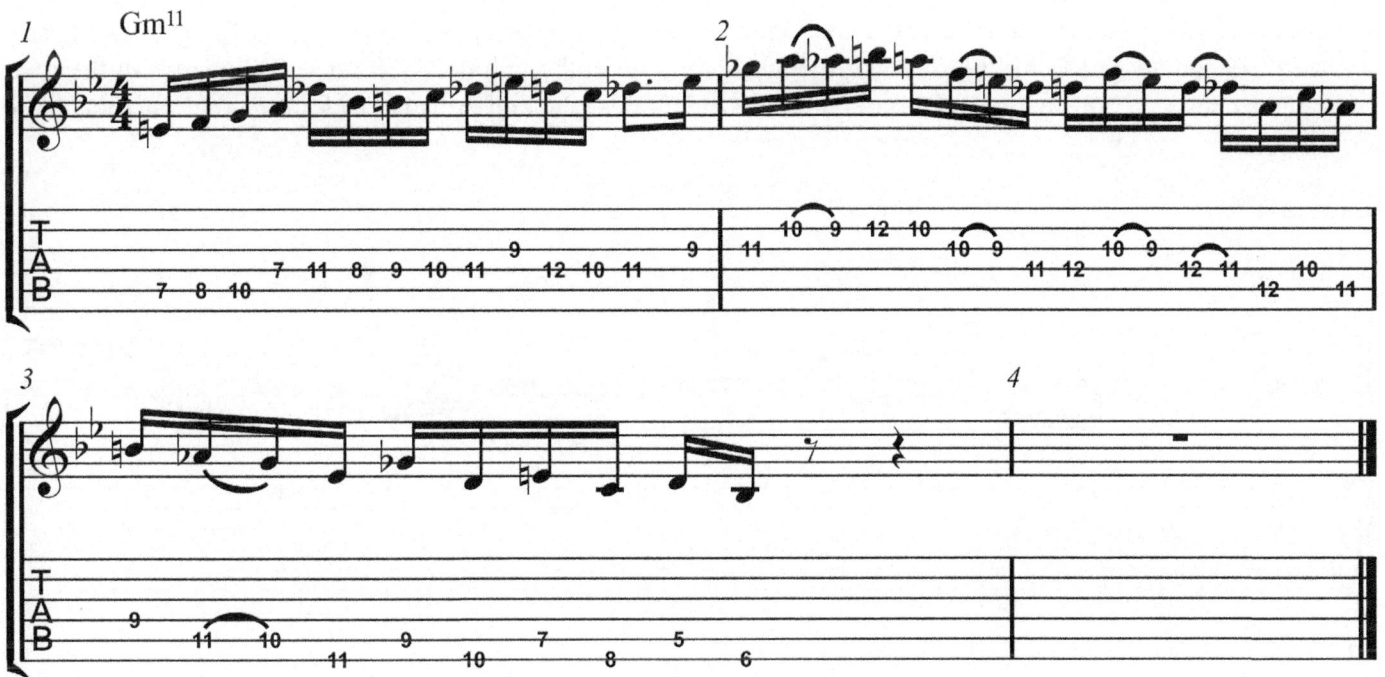

This idea is relatively straightforward and sticks mainly to notes from G Melodic Minor. The wide octave leaps in the second bar suggest FMaj7 and BbMaj7 arpeggios, while the end of the second bar contains the major 3rd (B) which implies G7.

Example 7f:

This idea uses a pattern similar to Example 7a and often crops up in McLaughlin's playing. Here, G Locrian is used to imply a Gm7b5 tonality over the Gm11 chord. The pattern shifts down a half-step to suggest a hybrid of G Ionian and G Mixolydian with some chromatic embellishment. The descending run in the final bar emphasises the E to suggest G Dorian, although the F# near the end pulls us back into a melodic/harmonic minor sound.

Example 7g:

Example 7h sticks mainly to notes from G Dorian. The second part of the lick uses G# Melodic Minor and outlines two dominant chords (C#7 and D#7) found within that scale.

Example 7h:

This line superimposes a C7 Pentatonic (1 3 4 5 b7) over G Minor. McLaughlin often used this scale with The Mahavishnu Orchestra and it is sometimes known as the "Jan Hammer scale". It was also part of Jeff Beck's sound in the mid-1970s when he played more Fusion-orientated music. When this scale is superimposed over Gm11 it creates a G Dorian sound but retains the C Dominant/Mixolydian flavour which offers a hint of an Indian vibe.

Example 7i:

Example 7j begins with G Melodic Minor ideas that include a #4 (C#) before a root-2-3-4 motif ascends chromatically. At the end of the 3rd bar, a descending "stair-step" lick is used in a similar way to Pat Metheny's melodic cell in Example 2d. McLaughlin, however, plays this idea on one string rather than two. The final phrase ascends G Minor Pentatonic with multiple chromatic embellishments and approach notes.

Example 7j:

In Example 7k we use a three-note motif similar to Example 7d. It initially appears to be Locrian but as the 1-2-4 fingering idea continues on each string, it develops into a more chromatic/symmetrical idea. The second half of the example uses a series of descending major and minor triads, largely from G Half-Whole, including Gb Major, E Minor, Bb Major, C# Minor, Eb Major and E Major.

Example 7k:

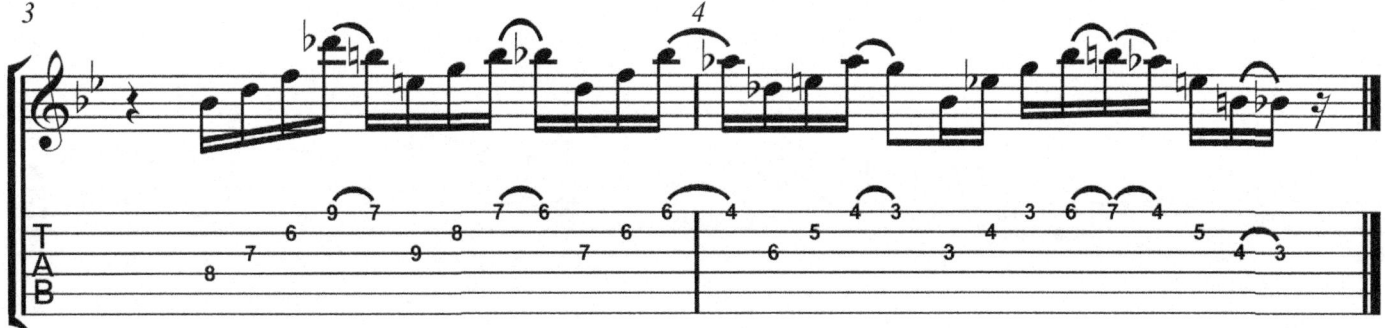

This diminished scale line is set up by an idea built around a G Minor triad. Notice how a motif from the G Half-Whole Diminished scale moves in minor 3rds beginning on the final beat of the first bar and continuing into the second. The line ends with a long, ascending six-note-per-string idea which requires strong, accurate alternate picking.

Example 7l:

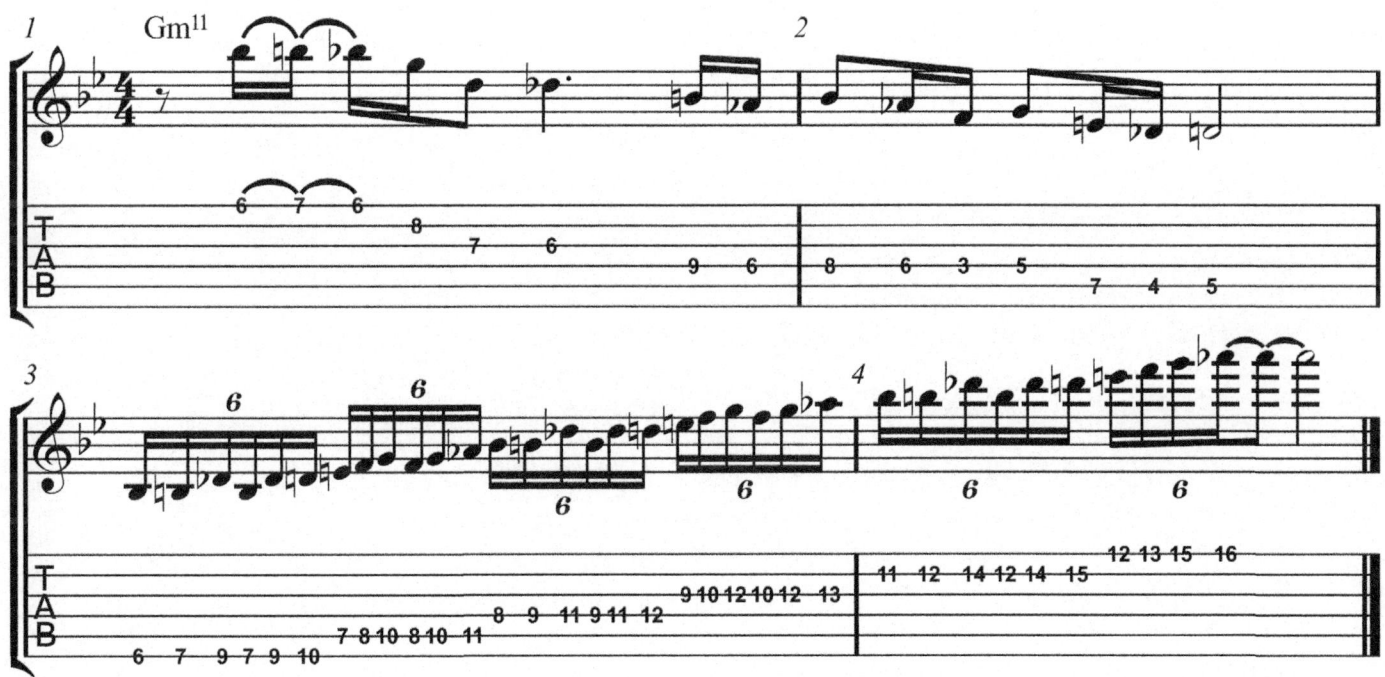

Our final line moves the concept from Example 7a around horizontally and vertically simultaneously, using six notes of G Half-Whole Diminished across three octaves to create a hexatonic scale. The line descends using a mixture of 3rds and 4ths, which are challenging to articulate due to the required combination of alternate picking and string jumps.

Example 7m:

Chapter Eight: Wayne Krantz

Wayne Krantz is originally from Corvallis, Oregon, where he was born on 26th July, 1956.

Inspired by The Beatles, Krantz took up the guitar at 14 and was drawn towards progressive Rock bands, particularly Jethro Tull and Chicago. He attended Berklee College of Music and has described his playing during this period as being heavily influenced by Pat Metheny.

During the 1990s, Krantz had a close association with Leni Stern and has played with Chris Potter, Donald Fagen and Billy Cobham. He favours a guitar trio line-up where he is free to improvise with more open-ended tonalities and structures. The albums *Long To Be Loose* (1993) and *Two Drink Minimum* (1995) showcase Krantz's unique musical approach, which he has since developed on *Howie 61* (2012) and *Good Piranha/Bad Piranha* (2014).

Krantz has been associated with the 1973 Fender Stratocaster pictured on his early solo albums but also uses Tyler and Suhr Stratocaster-style guitars. He tends to downplay the importance of specific equipment beyond the guitar itself, generally favouring generic rather than boutique amps.

As always, let's begin by looking at some idiomatic features of Krantz's playing.

Example 8a uses the G Whole-Half Diminished scale to demonstrate Krantz's use of syncopation and space. Where many players play dense lines of continuous 1/16th notes, Krantz tends to make use of different rhythms to create interest. The 1/8th note rests on beat 1 and throughout the phrase places the 1/16th notes on off-beats.

Example 8a:

Example 8b shows one way in which Krantz uses superimposition. Here, a Cm7b5 arpeggio is played over Gm to introduce the 4, b6, b3 and 7.

Example 8b:

Krantz often uses open strings as melody notes. Here's a G Dorian run, but every time an open string is available it is played instead of a fretted note. This creates a lovely texture and is an approach also used by Bill Frisell.

Example 8c:

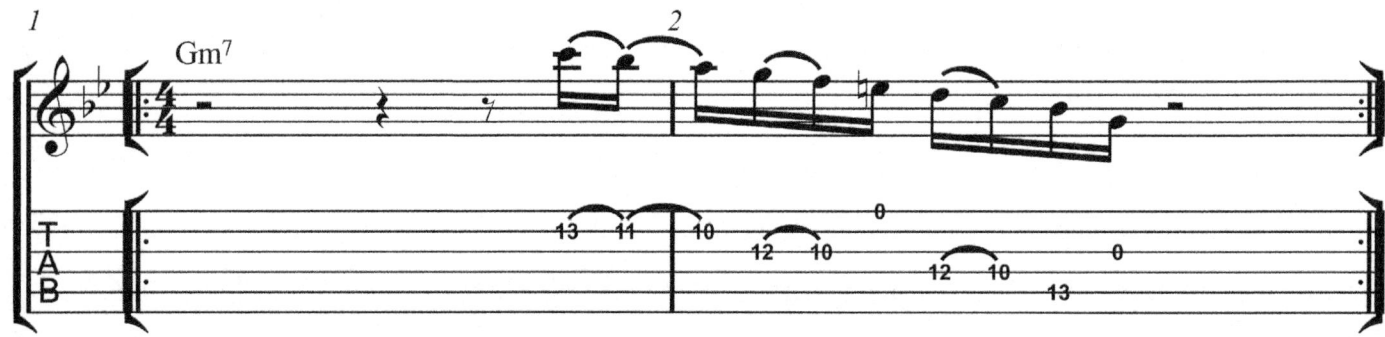

Example 8d looks at another popular Krantz sound, the Whole Tone scale. Here, we use chromatic passing notes to bridge the two-fret gaps between each scale note, which breaks up the symmetrical nature of the scale.

Example 8d:

This idea is built around G Dorian with some chromatic passing tones. The 1/16th note rests add rhythmic variety and lend a funky quality to a line that works particularly well on a Stratocaster. The example makes use of the lower strings for a darker texture.

Example 8e:

Example 8f further explores the lower registers of the guitar. This is an example of how Krantz might use a melodic cell of three or four notes that is moved in parallel. It explores melodic and rhythmic possibilities while moving between scale tones to create consonance and chromatic dissonance.

Example 8f:

Here we superimpose a bluesy chromatic C7 line over Gm7 in the first two bars. This C Mixolydian over G Minor approach is essentially a G Dorian line, but with a different emphasis from thinking "G Minor". The second half uses open string pull-offs in the manner of a Country or Rock player, but with a tight, funky rhythm. Make sure the 1/16th notes are even, controlled and clearly articulated.

Example 8g:

Example 8h uses open strings in G Dorian and rapidly ascends the fretboard in sextuplets. Again, the challenge is to maintain even articulation across the entire line. The pentatonic phrase that ends the line includes more 1/16th note rests to create additional syncopation.

Example 8h:

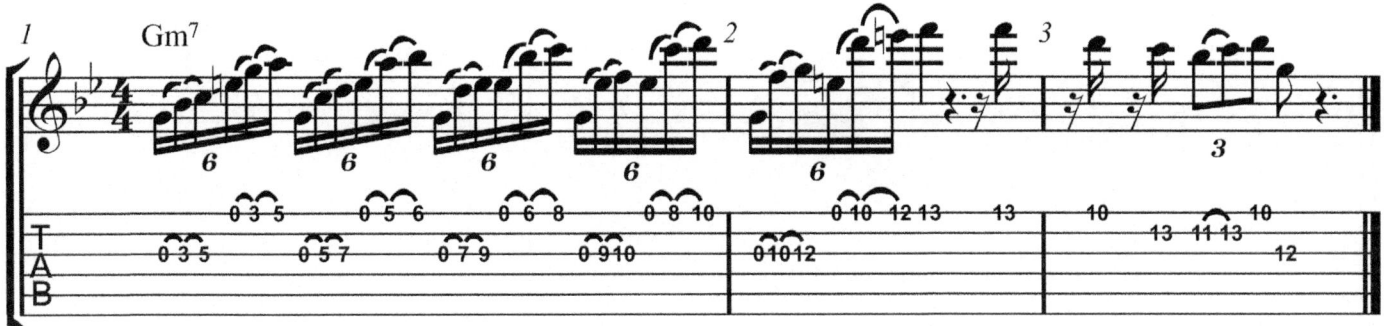

Example 8i starts with a conventional Jazz-Fusion 1/16th note phrase, but the repeated figure in bar two jumps octaves twice – a concept that adds an unusual twist to the phrasing and contour of the line. The final bar returns to more conventional phrasing.

Example 8i:

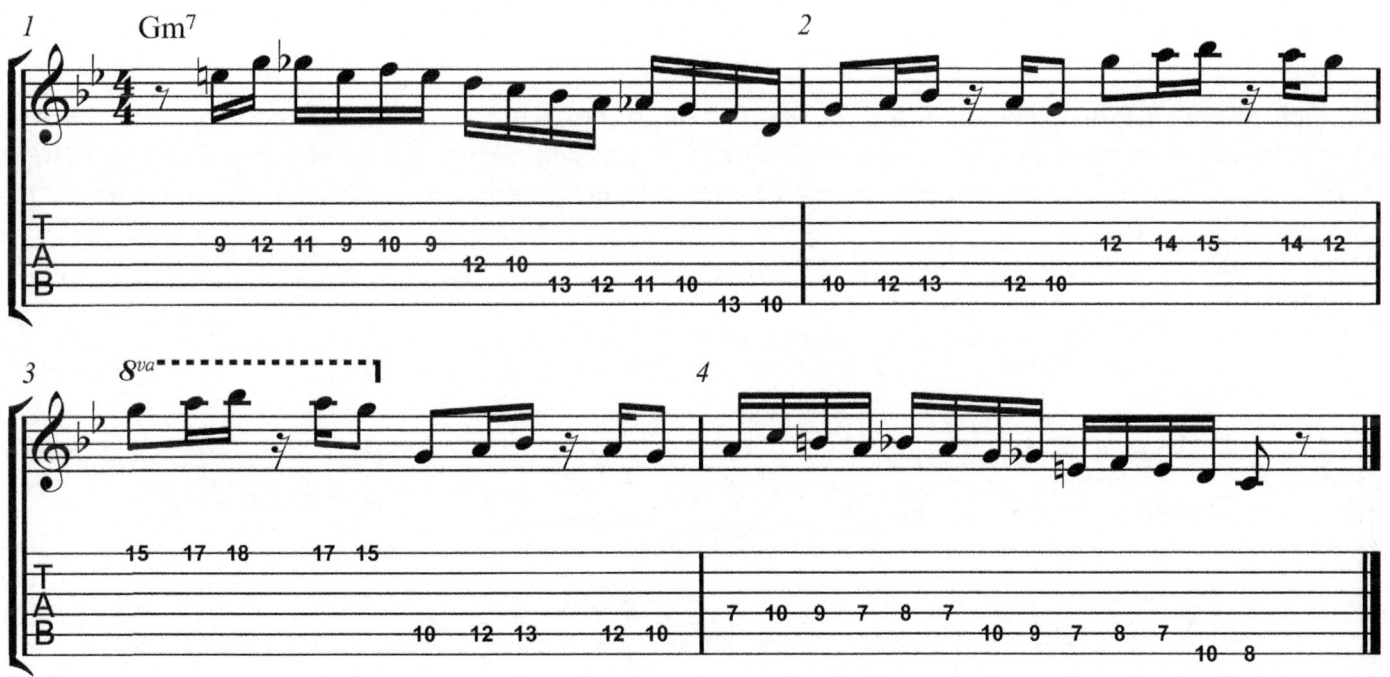

Choppy stop-start rhythms and a G Whole-Half Diminished scale played over Gm7 generate considerable tension here. The note choices are broadly Eb7alt, superimposed over Gm7, which resolve to a stacked 4ths idea.

Example 8j:

Example 8k comes from Bb Whole Tone. The main cell is constructed from an Augmented 7 arpeggio which is moved around in whole steps. The line descends horizontally until it reaches the 3rd position, where the Whole Tone scale is explored across the fretboard. Some chromatic embellishments are used to vary the predictable melodic nature of scale.

Example 8k:

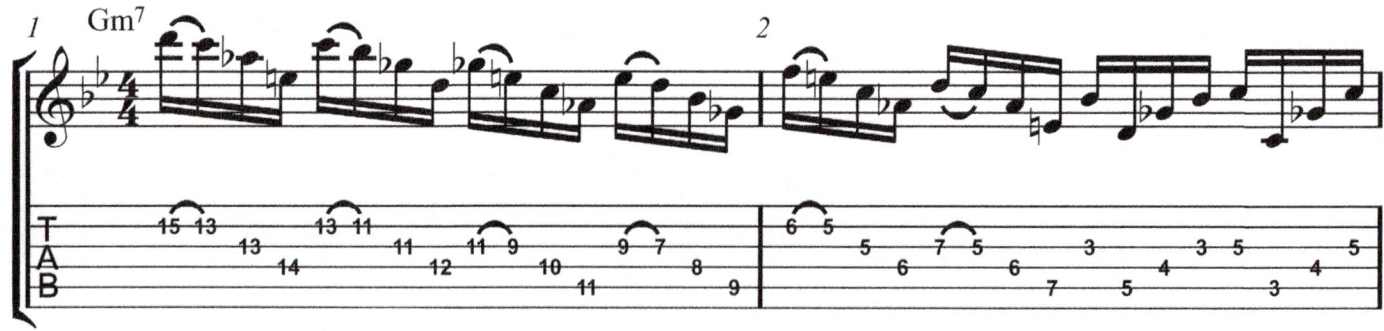

Example 8l uses G Whole-Half Diminished but with slightly unusual fingerings to create less predictable melodic phrasing. The first two bars hover between F#m7b5 and F#7 as a side-step from the G Minor tonality. After descending through the territory outlined in the opening bars, an open-string legato idea brings the example back to G Minor.

Example 8l:

Example 8m superimposes a Cm7b5 arpeggio over Gm7 to create a Gm(Maj7)#5 sound. The example crosses the neck to resolve to the tonic with some double octave intervals at the end.

Example 8m:

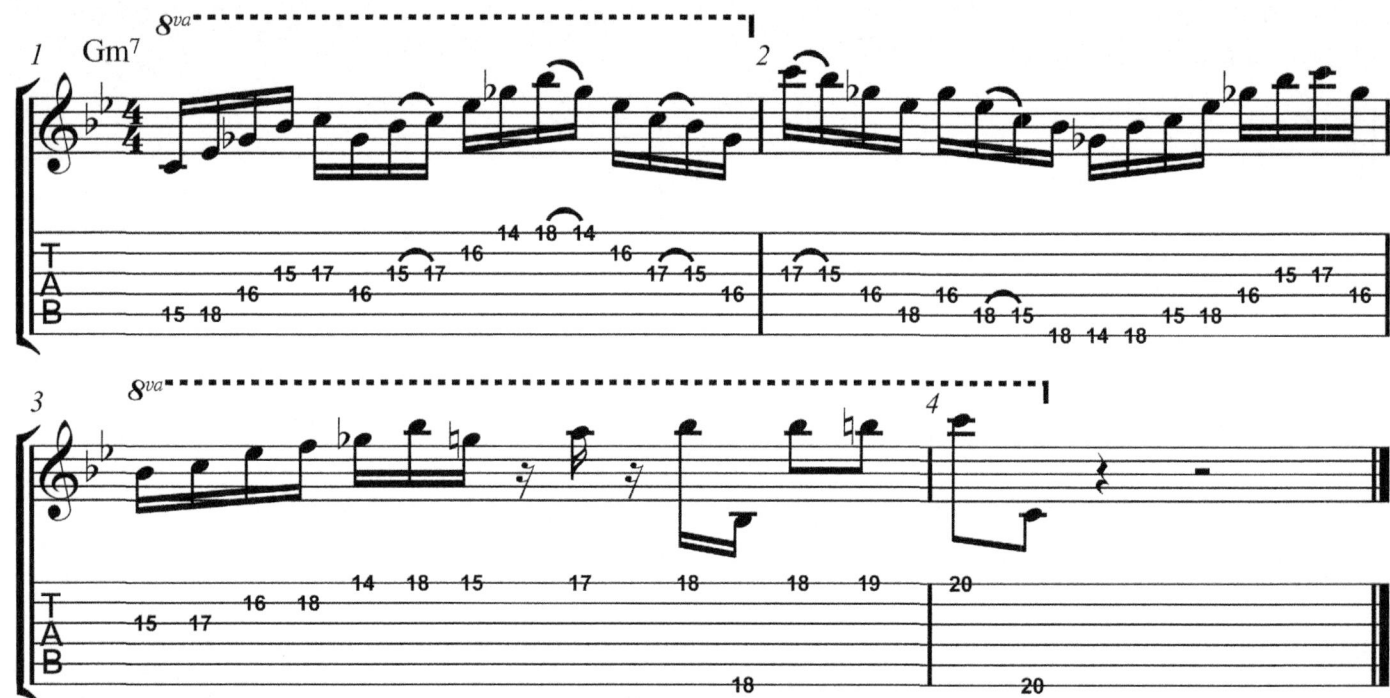

Example 8n moves a first inversion minor triad around in parallel by tracing a D Minor Pentatonic scale with the highest note of each triad. Note how the highest note outlines a melody of F, D, C, A, G, F, D. The example stays largely with G Dorian despite the parallel movement, but Eb (b13) and Ab (b9) notes do occur. The line ends with a Dm7 arpeggio to create a Gm11 sound over the harmony.

Example 8n:

Chapter Nine: Jimmy Herring

Jimmy Herring was born in Fayetteville, North Carolina, on January 22nd, 1962, and picked up the guitar when he was 13. Playing in Jazz and Fusion bands at school, he attended the Guitar Institute of Technology in Hollywood, California.

Herring started his life as a professional musician playing with Col. Bruce Hampton and The Aquarian Rescue Unit, who were jam bands in the late 1980s and early 1990s. These bands combined the long form jams of hippy-era bands like the Allman Brothers Band and The Grateful Dead, with Funk grooves in the style of The Meters and Funkadelic.

Throughout the 1990s Herring toured with various incarnations and spin-offs of the Grateful Dead, including Phil Lesh and Friends, The Dead and The Allmans. Herring's reputation grew between the '90s to '00s and he played in many bands including Jazz Is Dead with Billy Cobham, Widespread Panic, and The Codetalkers.

His 2008 debut album *Lifeboat* featured Derek Trucks, along with The Burbridge Brothers, Oteil and Kofi. Herring's second solo album *Subject to Change Without Notice* cemented his reputation as a key player in the Fusion, Blues and Rock scenes, and he was featured on the cover of *Guitar Player* magazine.

In the last decade, Herring has collaborated with top Fusion guitarists such as Wayne Krantz and Michael Landau in The Ringers, and with John McLaughlin in 2017. One of Herring's latest projects is "The 5 of 7" which features Kevin Scott and Rick Lollar.

His main guitar is a modified American Fender Stratocaster with two Lollar humbuckers, but he uses various PRS, Gibson and Telecaster guitars too. He favours Fender Super Reverbs, Marshall Super Leads and Fuchs amps with Tone Tubby cabs.

Let's begin our look at Jimmy's style with some idiomatic examples of his approach.

Example 9a is derived from a diminished chord shape and adds an approach note from a half-step below. The string skip between the D and B strings is repeated on the G and E strings a b5 higher and the structure is moved around the neck in minor 3rds.

Example 9a:

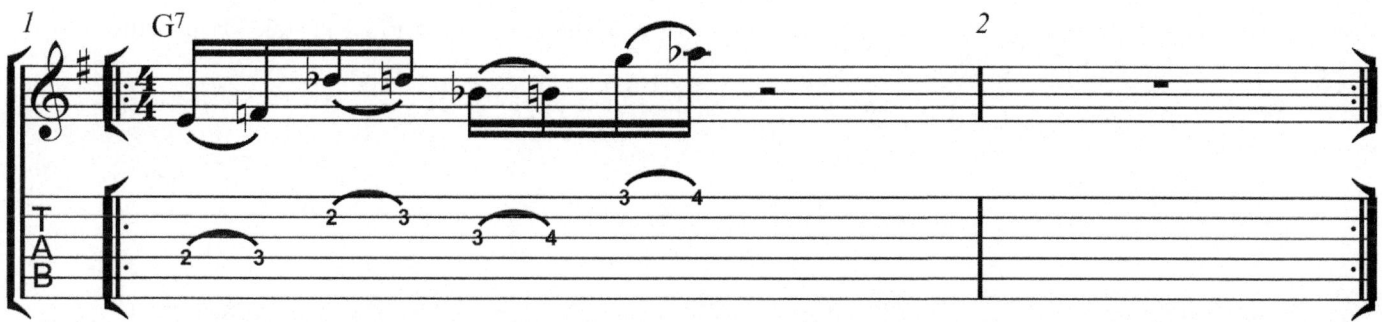

This cell demonstrates how the diminished scale contains bluesy dominant and minor pentatonic fragments that can be moved around the neck in minor 3rds. Try omitting the final note, then loop this idea as a triplet rhythm to create a useful, rapid fire-triplet idea.

Example 9b:

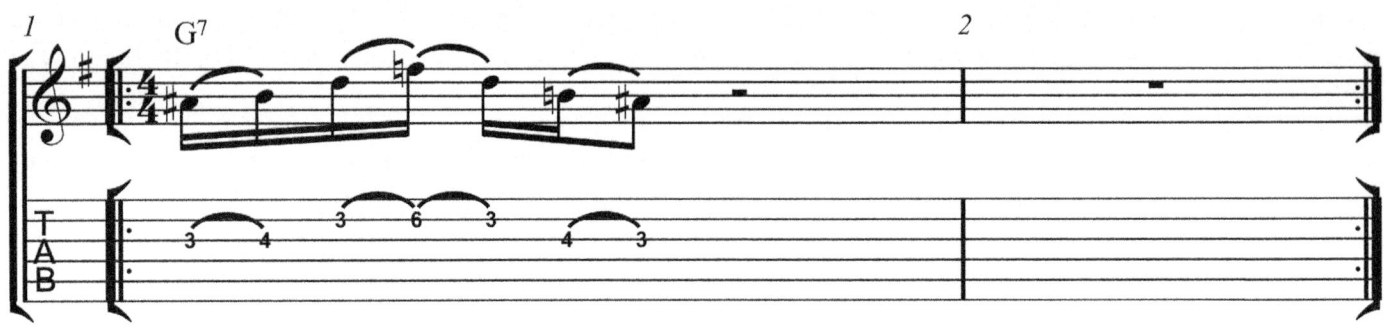

Example 9c focuses on Herring's faux-slide stylings, an essential part of his Southern Fusion style. This Derek Trucks-style idea creates a slide guitar texture without using a slide. The fast, consecutive grace-note slides combine with the final note played by sliding from the 8th to the 11th fret, before choking the note for a dramatic pause. This *capping* of the phrase adds to the slide articulation and is a hallmark of players such as Trucks and John Mayer.

Example 9c:

This idea demonstrates Herring's use of intervallic shapes. This example combines 5ths, 9ths and 11ths to create an angular yet melodic statement. These intervals are challenging to play, so take your time and try expanding the idea through different scales.

Example 9d:

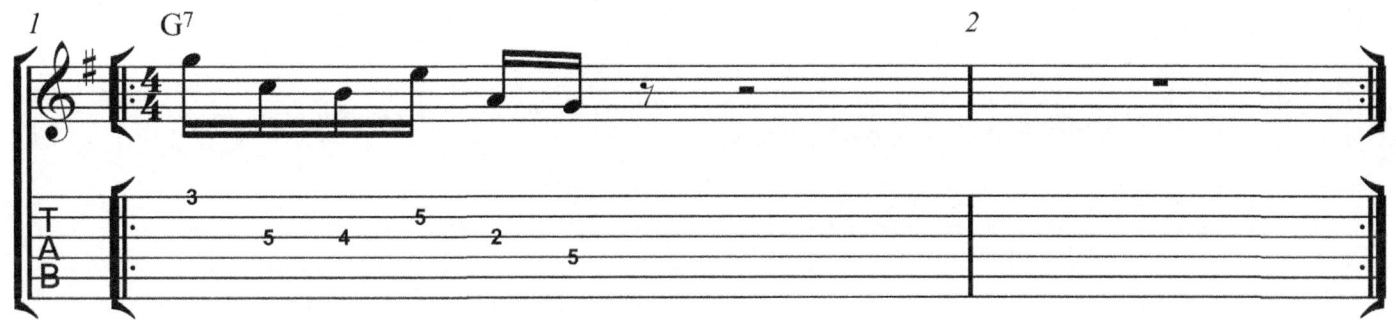

Our first phrase uses the concept in Example 9a and moves the diminished motif up to the 8th/9th position, where a bluesy B.B. King style lick completes the phrase. A *micro-bend* on the last note of this line would squeeze even more attitude out of the phrase.

Example 9e:

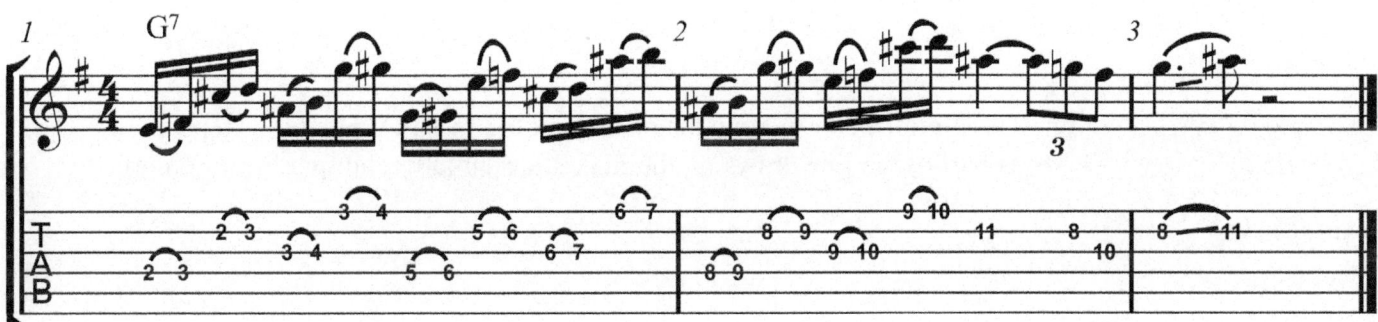

Example 9f is in two parts. Both parts use G Half-Whole Diminished, but the first part focuses on creating a bluesy vibe with two-note-per-string phrases. Bar one ends with E Major, G Major, C# Major and A# Major triads that are found within the scale. The second part of the lick is a common descending pattern which ends in some bluesy stylings.

Example 9f:

Example 9g takes a common G Diminished arpeggio shape and moves in half and whole steps alternately to cover all eight notes. The final part of the line draws on the faux slide-guitar technique from Example 9c.

Example 9g:

Example 9h is a dense 1/16th note G Half-Whole line somewhat reminiscent of John McLaughlin. A combination of alternate picking and pull-offs allows both rhythmic assertiveness and smooth execution. The melodic pattern from Example 9a is used, but this time descending into a short minor pentatonic phrase.

Example 9h:

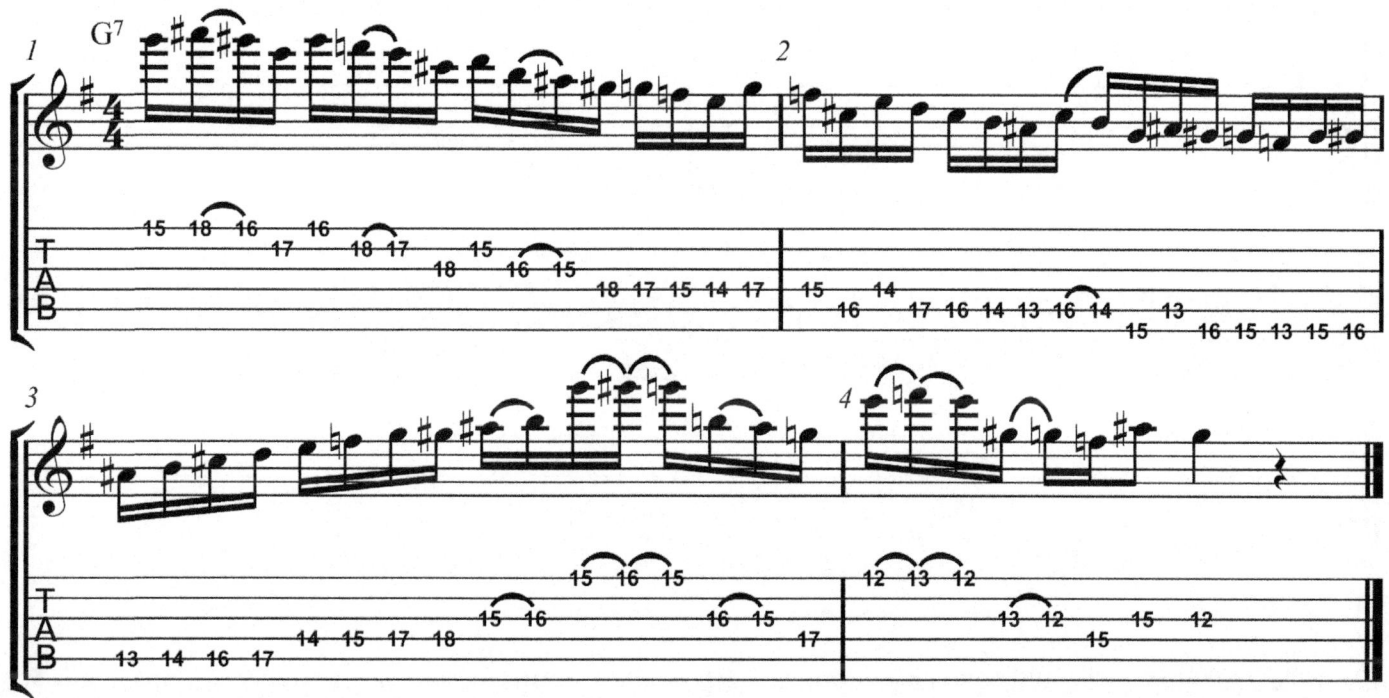

Here's a bluesy Duane Allman-like idea. After the first bend, notice how the lick slides from the 5th to the b5 to create a bottleneck texture before resolving to the 3rd and root. The second half of the lick uses an intervallic phrase based around 4ths that descend in minor 3rds.

Example 9i:

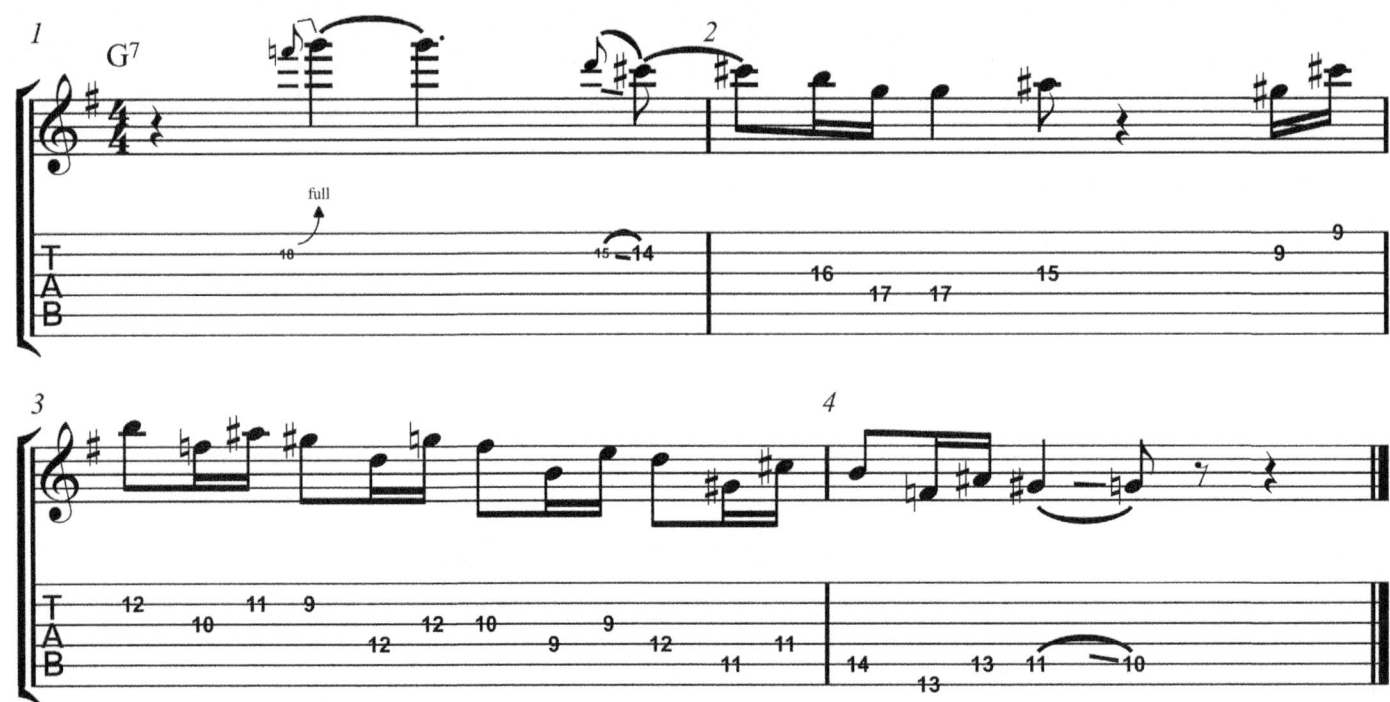

Example 9j explores a Whole Tone idea within G Half-Whole Diminished. After four transpositions, the four-note motif ascends through A# Major, E7 and G7 arpeggios before finally ending in G Major Pentatonic.

Example 9j:

The sixth note in this ascending G Minor Pentatonic run is played twice and is approached by a half-step below. The note is then bent up by a half-step to meet the pitch of the preceding note and the motif is repeated on the B and E strings respectively. The final bar consists of a descending G Minor Dorian/Pentatonic hybrid scale with chromatic passing notes.

Example 9k:

This eight-note G Half-Whole pattern is repeated three times and shifts positions using the first finger after each group of eight notes. The pattern descends from the 13th fret using a triplet figure which repeats symmetrically five times until it reaches the G tonic.

Example 9l:

Example 9m takes the intervallic 5ths concept from Example 9d and extends it further. This time we start high up the neck and move down in 2nds and 5ths. The second half of the line connects two pentatonic box positions.

Example 9m:

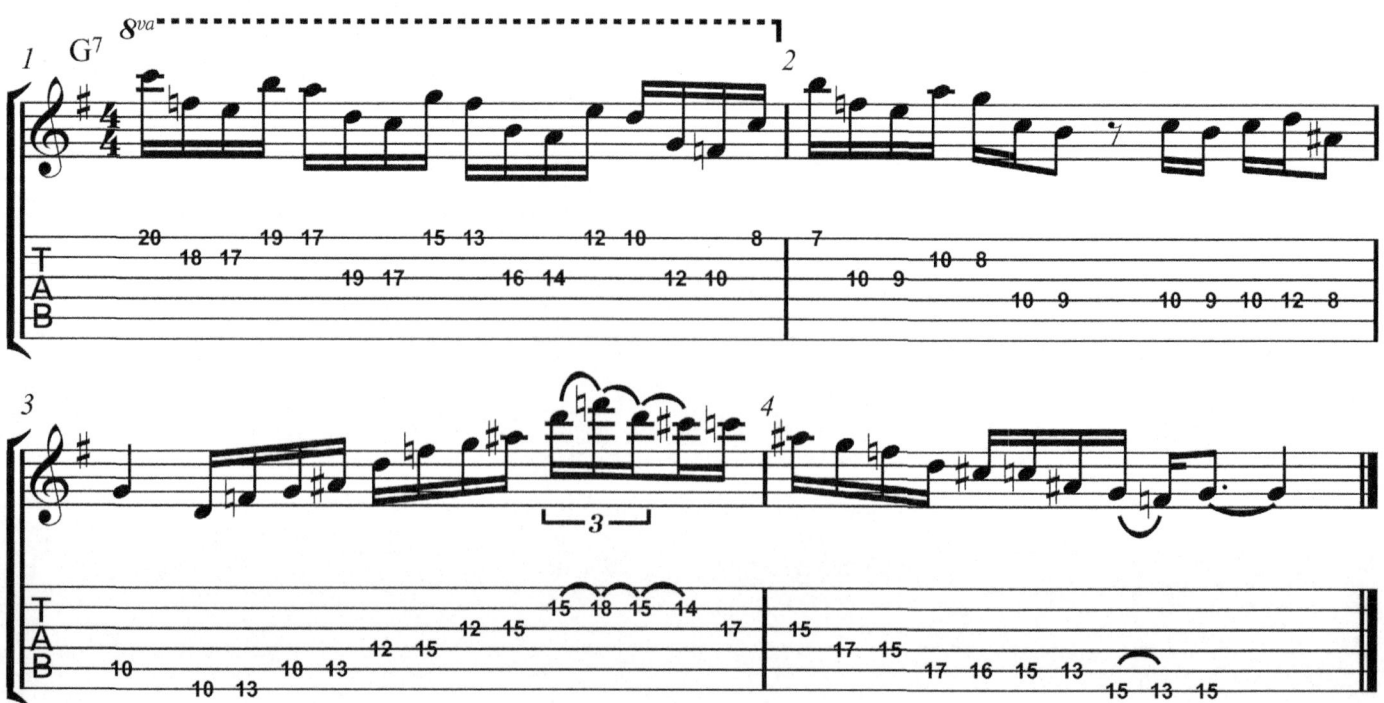

The final line combines the melodic cell structures of examples 9a and 9b with figures constructed from G Half-Whole Diminished. The first two bars create tension as the line ascends the neck to the tonic on the G string. Bar three is essentially the motif from Example 9a played with an emphatic major-sounding B.B. King blues phrase to conclude proceedings.

Example 9n:

Chapter Ten: Fusion Over II-V-Is

Our final section combines the concepts from previous chapters into lines you can play over both static grooves and jazzy chord changes. We have already seen how harmonic motion can be superimposed over static harmonic backgrounds to create interest, and especially common is to imply a V7-I sound, which we will explore further here.

In Jazz, there is often constant modulation. However, common Rock phrases can be adapted and adjusted to fit chord changes with interesting results. In this way, a fusion of Rock and Jazz styles can be achieved via Rock phrasing combined with Jazz theory, rather than simply using Jazz phrasing with a Rock tone.

In traditional Rock music, chord progressions and keys tend to be static or structured, so that little or no modulation is required. This makes long sequences easier to play as no adjustment to fit chord or key changes is required. However, here we will explore how to convert these types of lines to fit over the common II-V-I Jazz chord sequence. We will begin with five examples in the key of G which use the chord sequence Am7 – D7alt – GMaj7.

The first idea uses arpeggios and legato to navigate the chord changes. Bar one is built around an Am7 chord embellished with the b7 and 9th for some jazzy flavour. The second bar superimposes Ab Major over the D7alt – a common *tritone* or *b5* substitution. The final two bars are an extended B Minor Pentatonic phrase played over the GMaj7 I chord. Playing a minor pentatonic scale on the 3rd of a tonic major chord is a common substitution.

Example 10a:

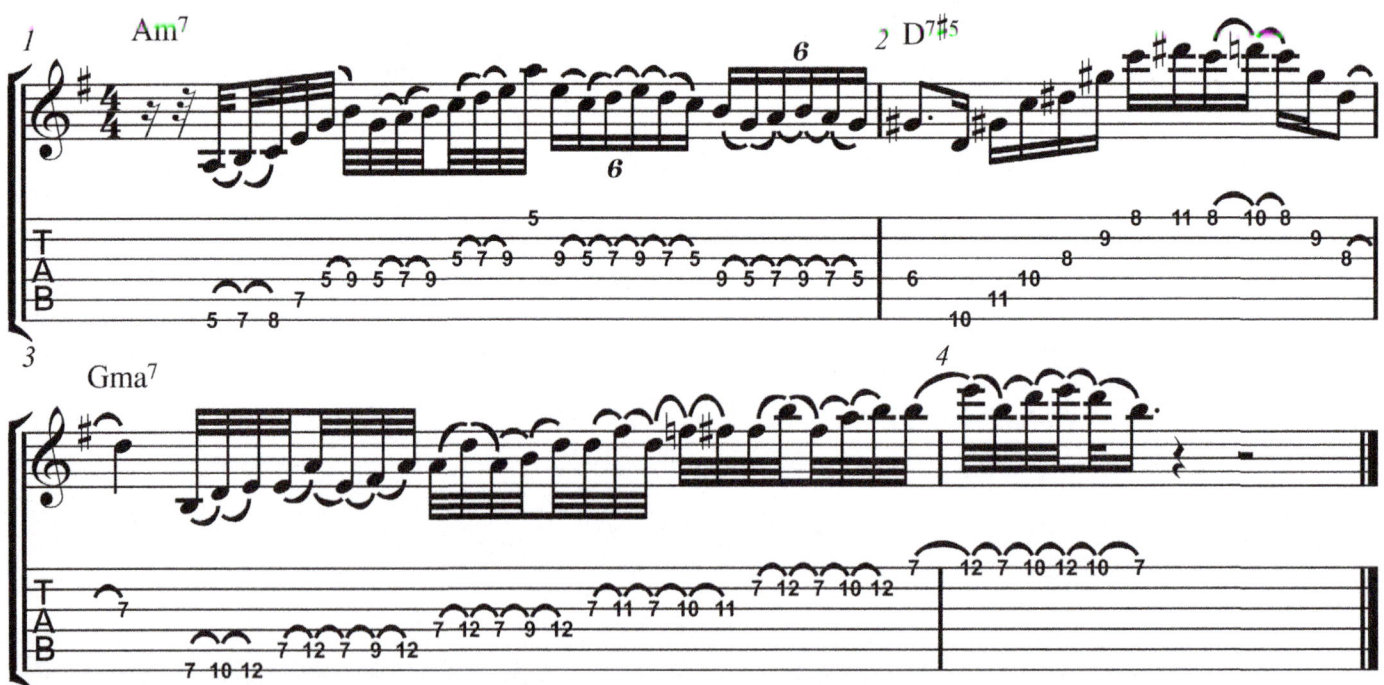

Example 10b uses wide 5th and 6th intervals over the II chord with descending slides and legato. On the D7 chord, I move to a three-note-per-string legato D Altered scale idea. Notice the extra note on each string that fills the gap between the scale tones. The final phrase on GMaj7 ascends through four positions of B Minor Pentatonic.

Example 10b:

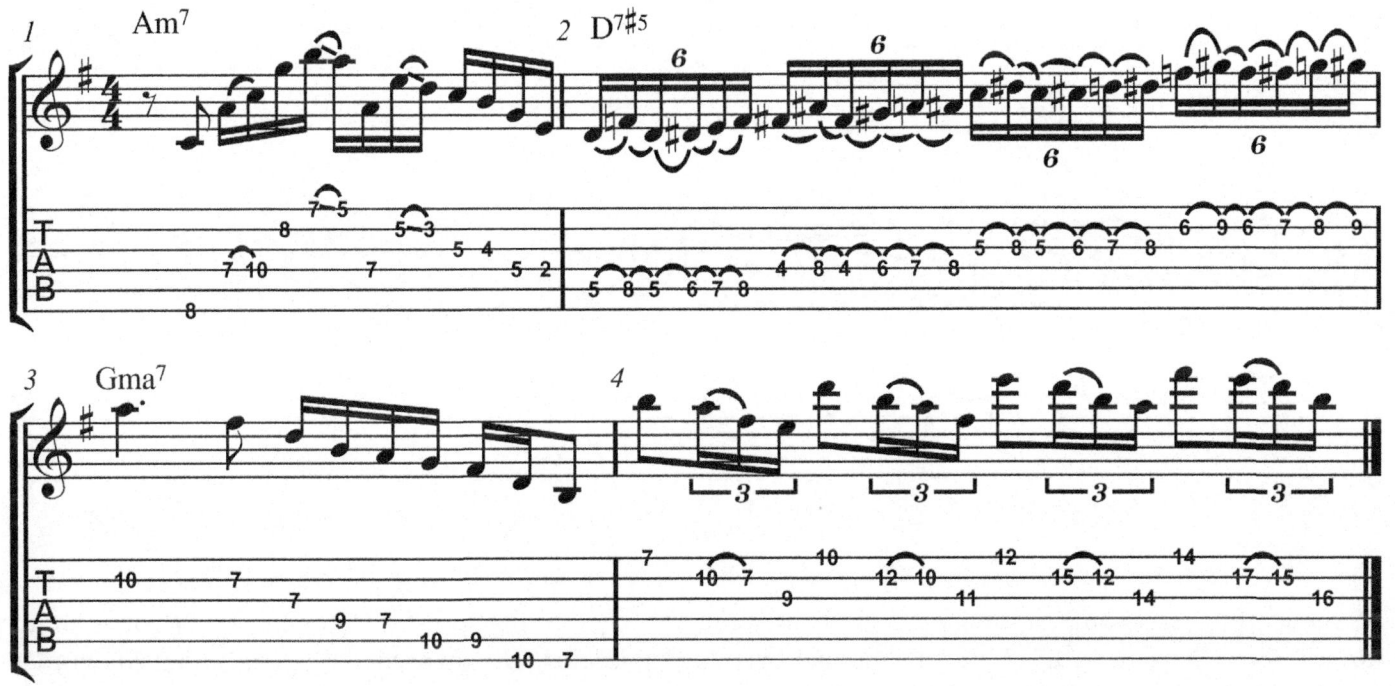

Example 10c uses the combination of an Am9 arpeggio and some "fill in the gaps" A Minor Pentatonic ideas on the higher strings, before it descends through the D Altered scale on the V chord. Again, a B Minor Pentatonic phrase is used over the GMaj7 chord.

Example 10c:

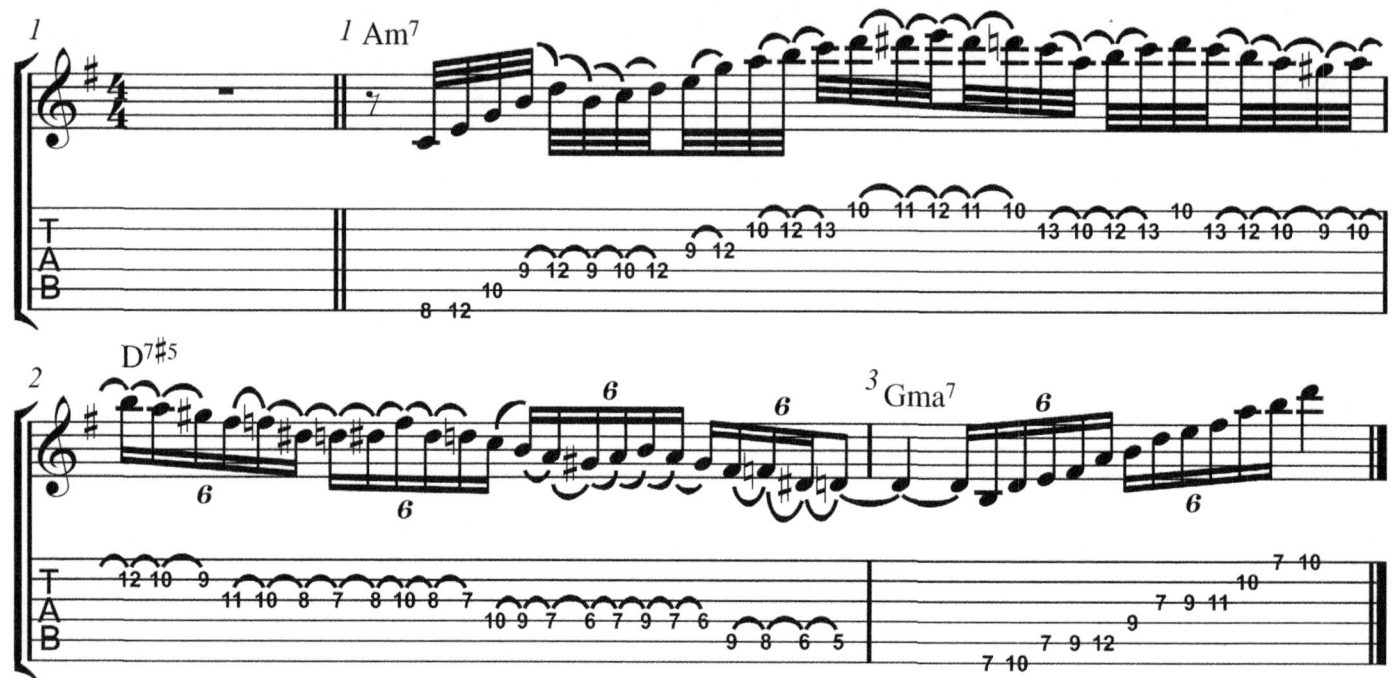

Example 10d adapts an Eric Johnson style pentatonic sequence to the II-V-I progression by articulating all three chords. Starting with E Minor Pentatonic over Am7 it begins with an ascending pattern that sometimes descends one note on a lower string. Each time this occurs, use a sweep to return to the higher string. Over the D7#5 I play F Minor Pentatonic which contains five of the seven notes of D Altered. The run ends on a B natural just before the bar line to anticipate the resolution to G Major.

Example 10d:

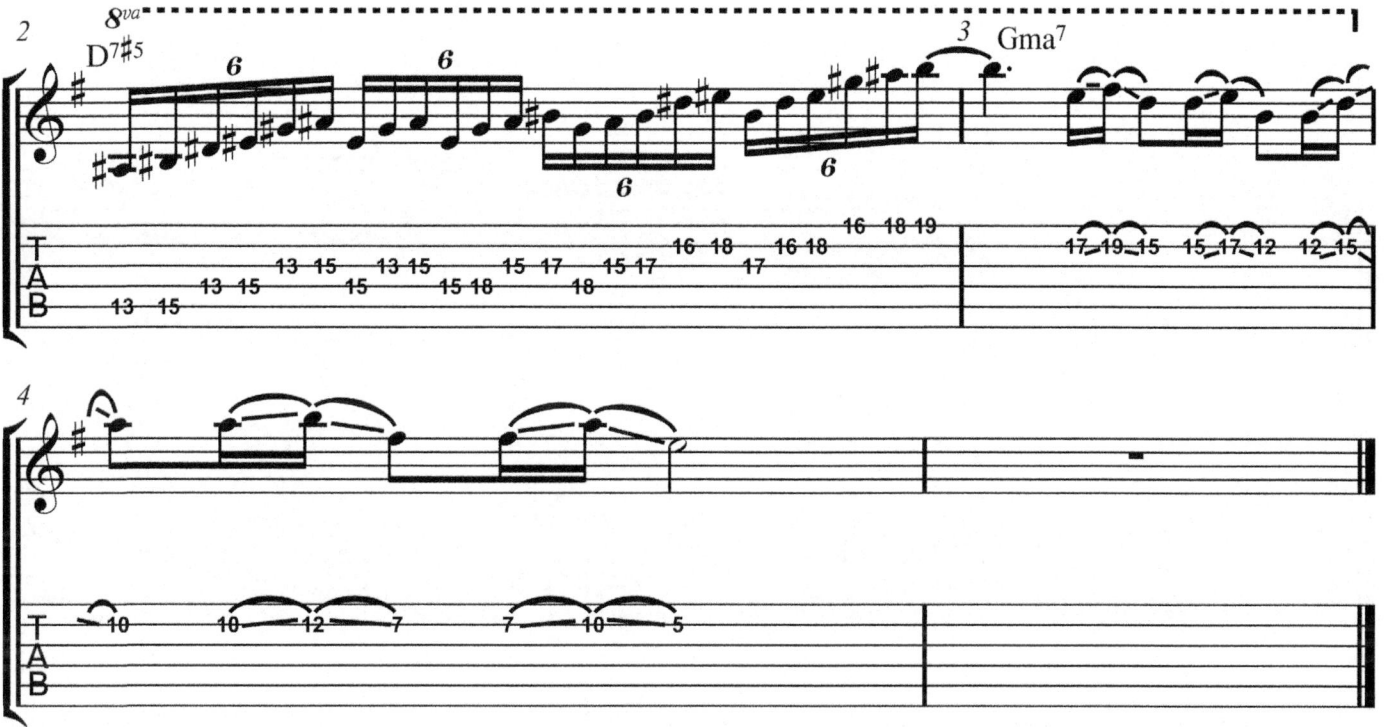

In the next line we again fill in the gaps between A Dorian scale tones over the II chord. This phrase then descends, after shifting up one position into D Altered in the second bar. The final phrase is reminiscent of 1980s shred players like Gary Moore and John Sykes.

Example 10e:

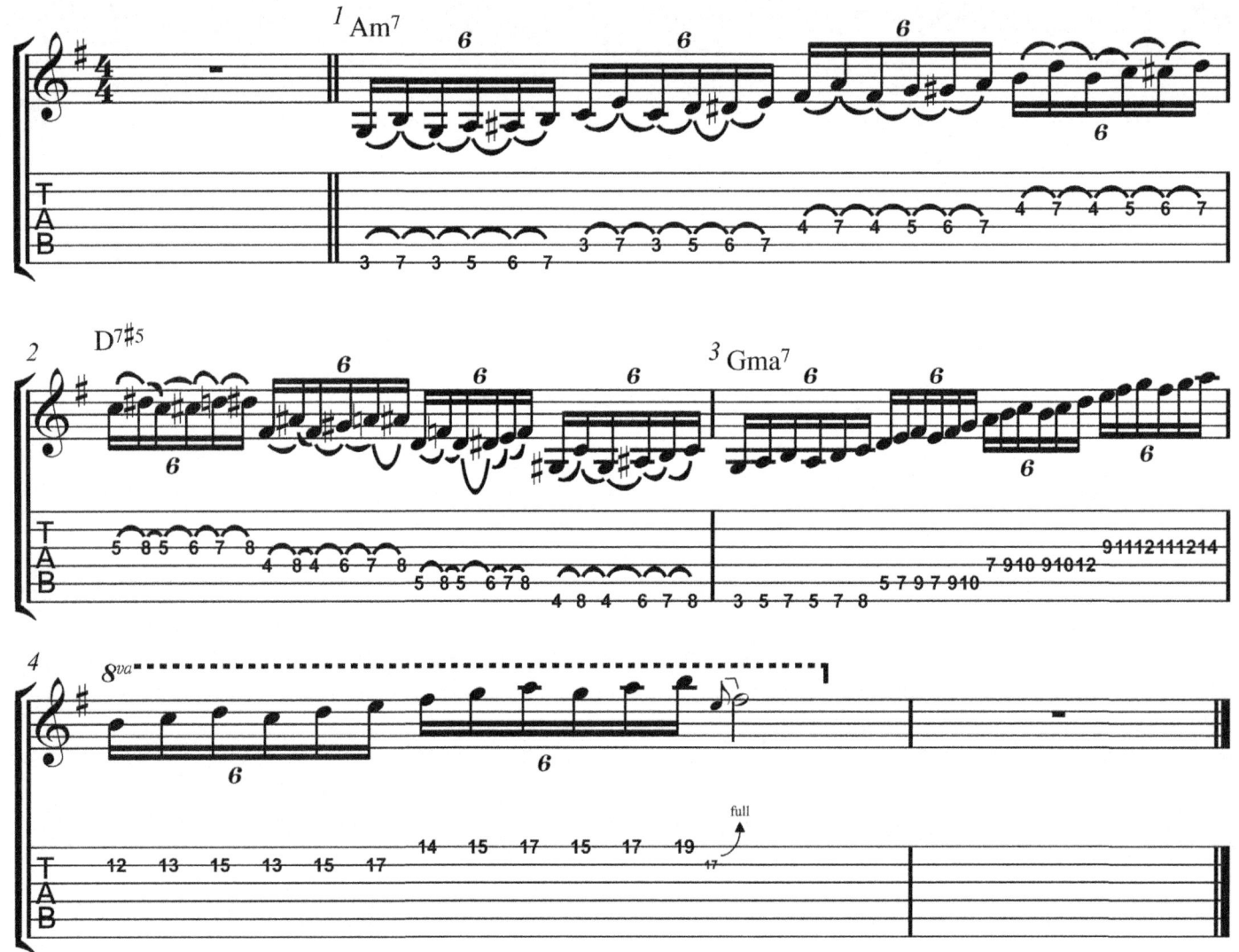

Now let's look at five examples that work over a Minor ii-V-i in G Minor: Am7b5 – D7b9 – Gm7 – Gm6.

The most common soloing choice for the Am7b5 ii chord is often A Locrian, although this chord is regularly ignored by improvisers who treat it as a "suspended" D7alt chord. If you play the notes of Am7b5 (A C Eb G) over a bass note of D, the resulting chord is D7b9sus4, which is so close to the following D7alt it can easily be ignored.

A common choice for the V7 (D7alt) chord is D Altered, although D Phrygian Dominant (a.k.a. G Harmonic Minor) is a very popular, if a little old-fashioned choice. As D Phrygian Dominant and G Harmonic Minor are essentially the same scale, it makes sense to play G Harmonic Minor over the whole Minor ii V i. However, again this is a little dated, and many players will often use a combination of G Dorian, G Minor Pentatonic and G Melodic Minor on the I (Gm7) chord.

The first Minor ii V i line requires economy or sweep picking for smooth execution and begins with five-note groupings of A Locrian in 1/32nd notes, but switches to sextuplets for the rest of the bar. In bar two we switch to three-note groups of D Altered. The lick ends with some bluesy minor pentatonic ideas with bends over the Gm7 and Gm6 chords.

Example 10f:

Here, the first bar alternates between groups of 1/16th notes and 1/16th note quintuplets in the style of Mahavishnu-era John McLaughlin, before switching to groups of fours and sixes more reminiscent of Al Di Meola's playing style.

The scale here is D Phrygian Dominant, which gives a more Spanish flavour. The final G Dorian run is again reminiscent of Al Di Meola, although it is a pattern commonly used by Rock and Metal players.

Example 10g:

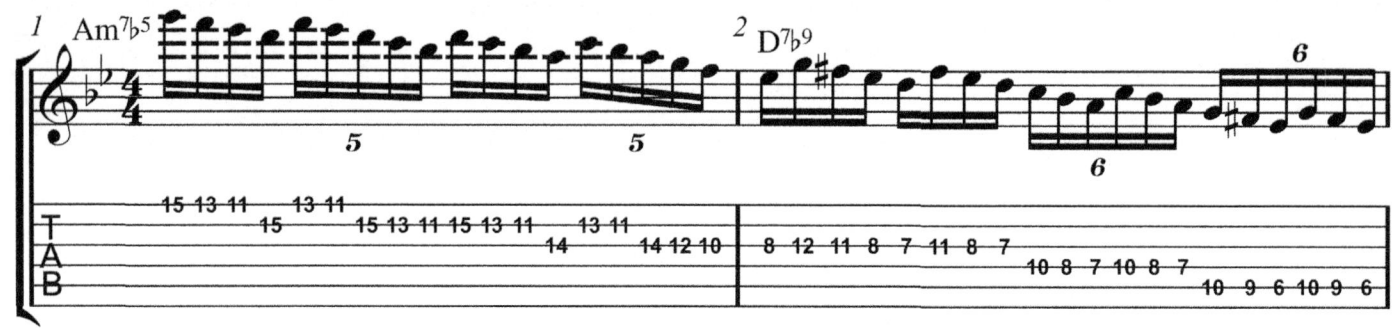

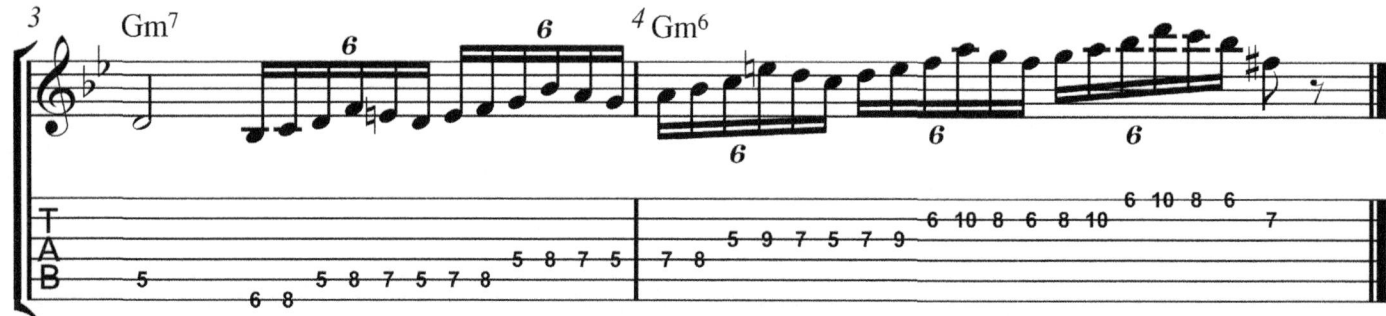

In Example 10h, we establish an eight-note pattern in 1/16ths which moves from A Locrian to D Half-Whole in the second bar. The first arpeggio over the i chord is Bbmaj7#11 which outlines G Dorian. The descending arpeggios in the final bar are from G Melodic Minor and combine Augmented and Major/Minor 7 sounds.

Example 10h:

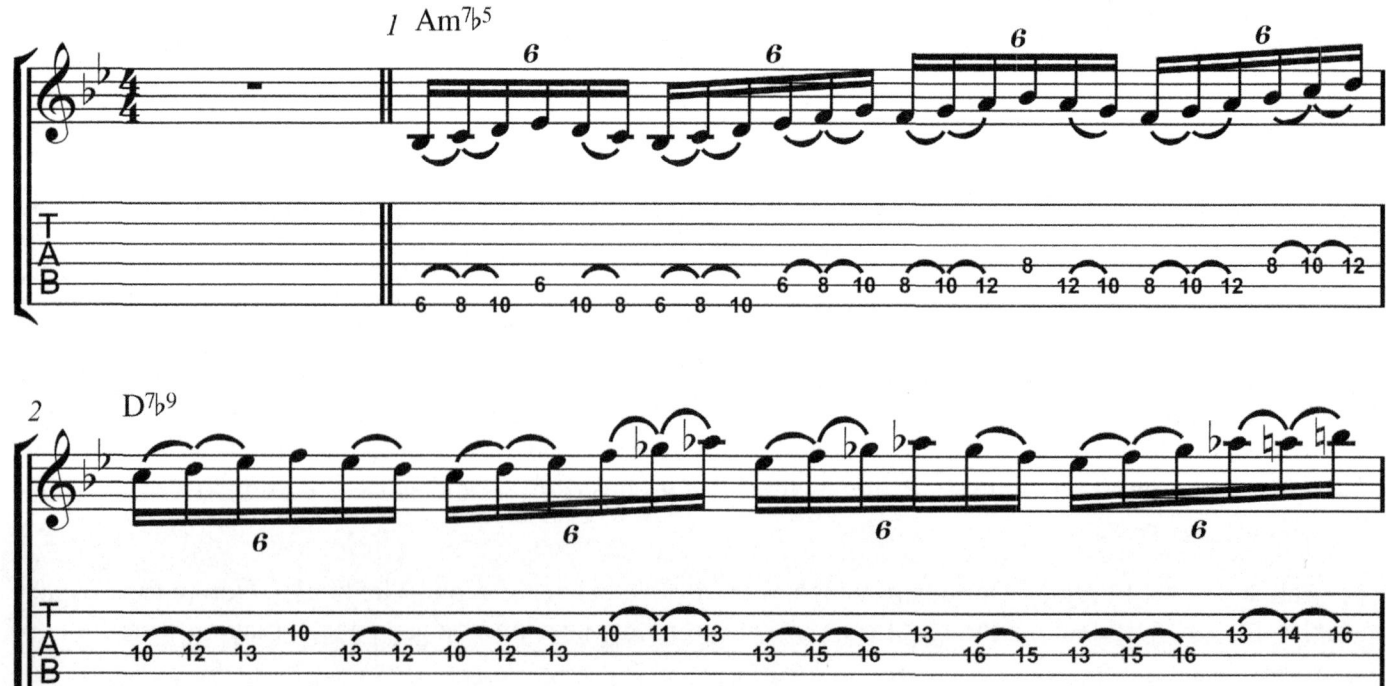

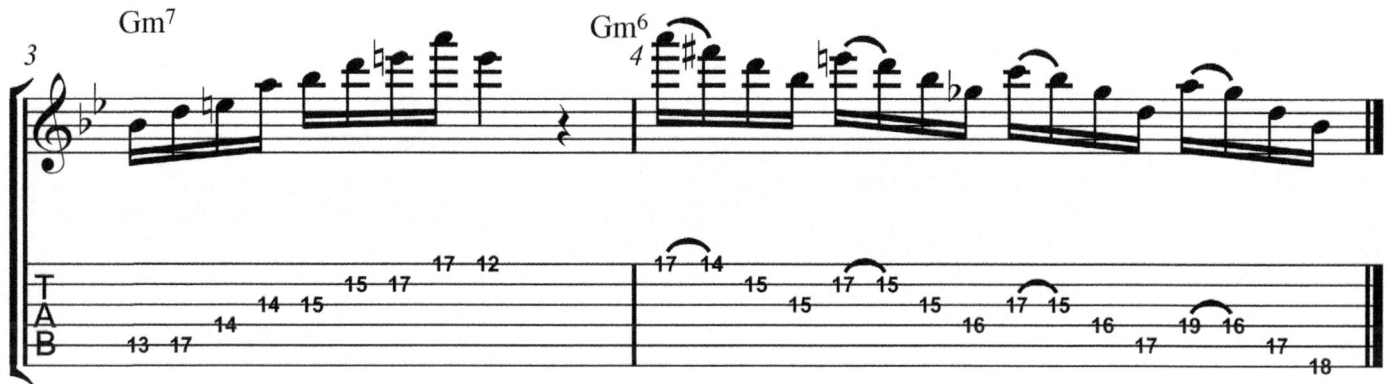

Next, an interesting tension is created by swapping between six- and five-note groupings. The scale over Am7b5 is A Locrian Natural 2nd, and over the D7b9 I play stretched Eb Diminished arpeggios with some Holdsworth-style string skipping. On the i chord, we zig-zag around G Melodic Minor.

Example 10i:

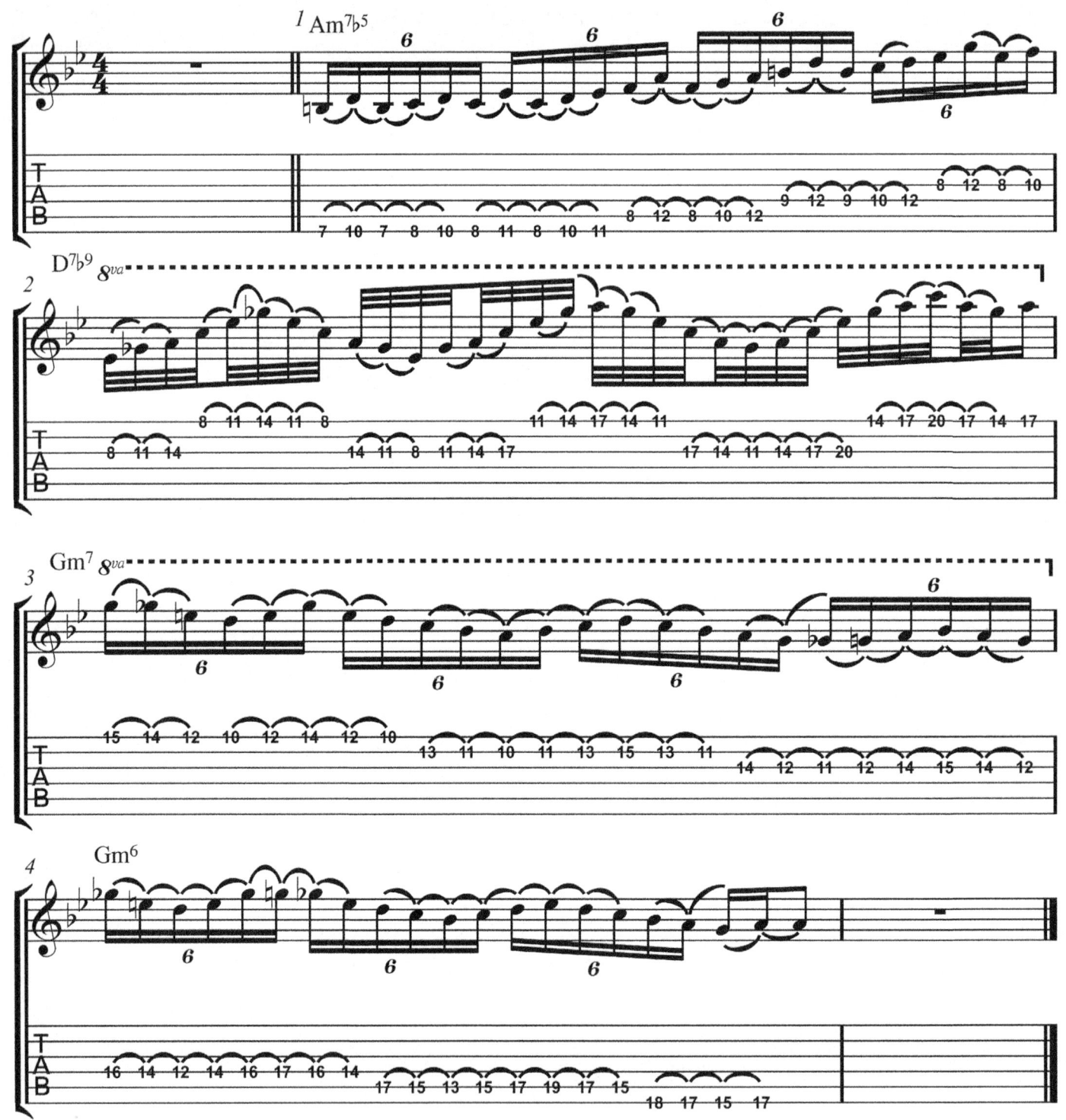

Finally, this Van Halen-style idea consists of three notes played legato that are then repeated and picked. This idea is repeated three times before switching to a Coltrane-style Augmented phrase over the D7b9 using a series of descending D Augmented triads. The final two bars are reminiscent of Steve Lukather, who uses many Fusion elements in his playing.

Example 10j:

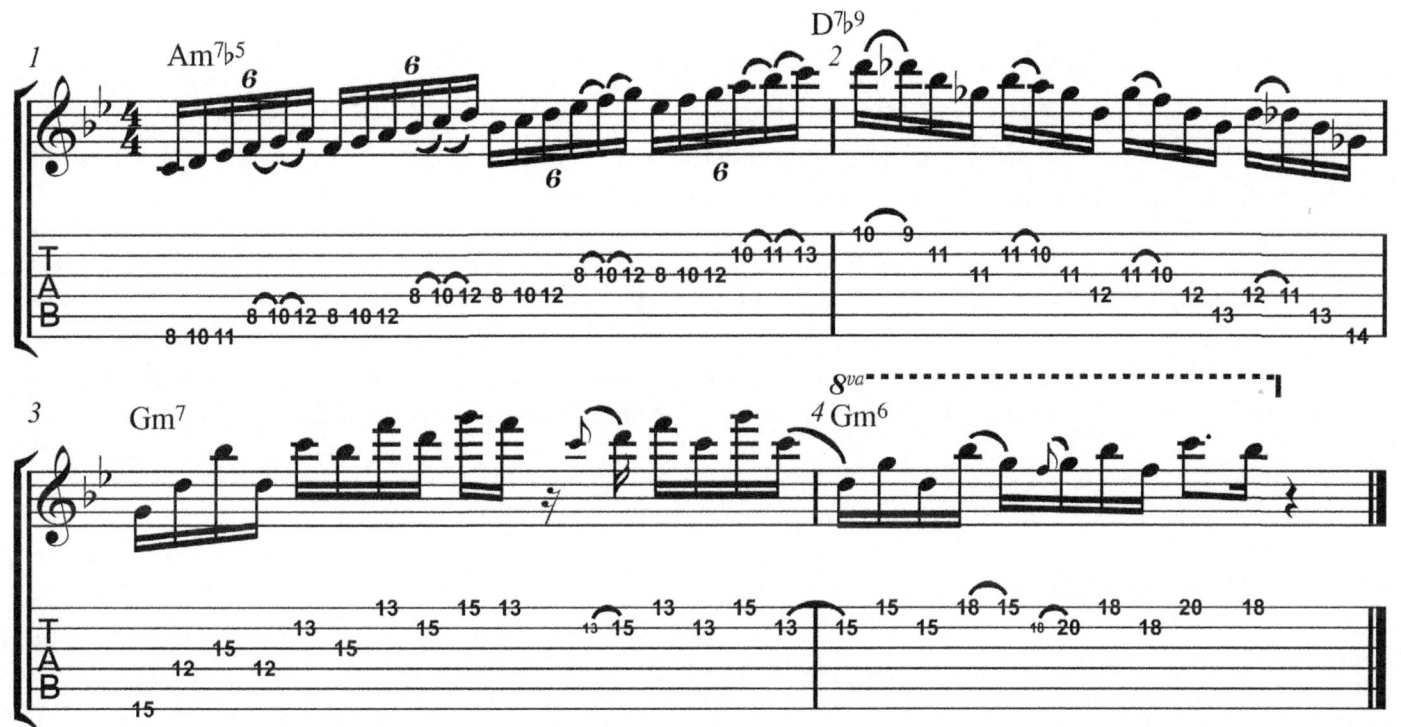

Conclusion

I hope you have found some useful material and inspiration in these 100 licks and that they help you find new creative directions by exploring the recordings of all the artists I've included.

Many of the harmonic ideas in Fusion take a while for the ear to become accustomed to. After all, one feature of Fusion can be its extreme dissonance and "controlled chaos". Developing your ears through active listening is crucial if you wish to use these sounds spontaneously in your own solos.

As a final note, I am aware that many players become hung up on theory and harmony when approaching Fusion, labouring under the misconception that they need to be able to justify every note they play through complex academic explanations. This is not true or helpful. All the players included here have their own idiosyncratic ways of viewing the guitar and its relationship to the music they play. Allan Holdsworth even had his own symbols for different scales and tonalities! Nothing is set in stone, and there are no rules to limit your exploration.

Remember, music always comes first, and analysis always comes after the event.

Good luck and all the best!

Nick Mellor

Printed in Great Britain
by Amazon